SIDNEY LANIER

The Man, the Poet, the Critic

SIDNEY LANIER

The Man
The Poet
The Critic

By Edd Winfield Parks

LAMAR LECTURES, WESLEYAN COLLEGE

University of Georgia Press · *Athens*

Foreword

SIDNEY LANIER—poet, critic, musician—was born in Macon, Georgia, on February 3, 1842. After the Civil War he lived for a time at Wesleyan College and while there met Mary Day, who became his wife.

It seemed thus appropriate for Wesleyan College to devote the 1968 Eugenia Dorothy Blount Lamar Lecture Series to Lanier. No one could have been a more fortunate choice of speaker for this series than the late Dr. Edd Winfield Parks. Dr. Parks might well be called the dean of Southern literary scholarship. A member of the English Department at the University of Georgia from 1935 until his death in 1968, he published a volume of poetry and fifteen other books. He taught in Brazil and Denmark on Fulbright professorships, and in 1958 traveled in several Latin American countries as a State Department lecturer.

The Eugenia Dorothy Blount Lamar Lecture Series at Wesleyan College was established by Mrs. Lamar to enable the college to bring to the campus each year a distinguished speaker on some aspect of Southern literature, history, and culture. This year Wesleyan College was honored to have Dr. Edd Winfield Parks as Lamar Lecturer on April 8 and 9.

Leah A. Strong
Professor of United States
Language and Literature

Wesleyan College
Macon, Georgia

Preface

THIS BOOK is an expansion of the Lamar Lectures delivered at Wesleyan College, Macon, in April 1968. It follows the plan of the three lectures (Lanier: Man, Poet, Critic), but I am grateful to President W. Earl Strickland and to Dr. Leah A. Strong, Professor of American Studies and Chairman of the Lamar Lecture Series Committee, for permission to add relevant and needed material that could not be encompassed in the one-hour talks.

I have listed the essential primary sources in a note on page 1; after that, I have used internal documentation, with some citations to other authors. In addition to those listed later, I have derived aid and insight from the scholarly studies of Philip Graham, Jay B. Hubbell, John Crowe Ransom, and numerous other writers. In the interests of consistency, I have followed Lanier's usage in spelling—for example, Shakspere. I have made no changes in direct quotations in his spelling and punctuation.

A shorter version of the second chapter appeared under the title "Lanier as Poet" in *Essays on American Literature in Honor of Jay B. Hubbell* (Duke, 1967). I am indebted to the Editor, Clarence Gohdes, and to the Director of the Duke University Press, Ashbel Brice, for allowing me to use this essay as the basis for the treatment of Lanier's poetry.

Two colleagues, John Olin Eidson and Rayburn S. Moore, read the typescript and made perceptive and useful suggestions. Ralph H. Stephens, Director of the University of Georgia Press, has been constantly helpful. Most of all, for steady encouragement and wise criticism I am grateful to my wife, Aileen Wells Parks.

Edd Winfield Parks

University of Georgia
Athens, Georgia

Contents

I The Man

SIDNEY CLOPTON LANIER was born in Macon, Georgia, February 3, 1842. His father, Robert Sampson Lanier, was a moderately successful lawyer, but his grandfather, Sterling Lanier, was reputed to be wealthy and owned hotels in Macon, in Montgomery, Alabama, and in the resort town of Montvale Springs, Tennessee. Lanier's mother, Mary Jane Anderson Lanier, was a lover of music, a skilled pianist, and a devout Presbyterian. The Laniers had once been French Huguenots who emigrated to England in Queen Elizabeth's time. Late in life Sidney believed himself a mystical throw-back to the Nicholas Lanier who composed the music for masques by Thomas Campion and Ben Jonson. The known facts of the life of this presumed ancestor (there are some gaps in the Lanier family tree) "seem to give some sort of legitimacy to my own passion for music" (X, 39).[1]

---

[1] Internal citations to the *Centennial Edition of the Works and Letters of Sidney Lanier*, ed. Charles R. Anderson et al. (10 vols.; Baltimore, 1945) are identified by volume and page numbers. References to Aubrey H. Starke's *Sidney Lanier* (Chapel Hill, 1933) and Edwin Mims's *Sidney Lanier* (Boston, 1905) will be given respectively as Starke and Mims, followed by the page number. *The Poems of Sidney Lanier* (1884) will be cited as *Poems*.

The Lanier home life seems to have been an extraordinarily happy one. Two more children were born to them, Clifford Anderson in 1844, and Gertrude (whom Sidney called Sissa) in 1848. Mrs. Lanier was more interested in her family than in society; many of their evenings were spent in reading aloud or in listening to her play the piano. When Sidney, about the age of five, was noticed accurately beating time to her playing, she bought for him an inexpensive flute on which he practiced "with the passion of a virtuoso." Soon he was making his own flutes out of river reeds, and improvising imitations of bird songs. He also learned to play the guitar, the piano, the organ, and the violin, which became his favorite instrument although his own playing practically ended when a window-sash fell, "fortunately taking off a half-inch only of a middle finger." He played in a juvenile minstrel band and led an orchestra composed of his playmates (C. A. Lanier, *Chatauquan*, XXI, 404–05).

The one rift in the family was over religion. Mr. Lanier had grown up a Methodist but at his wife's urging he attended the Presbyterian Church, although apparently more to keep harmony in the family than out of religious conviction. After Sidney had joined the Presbyterian Church, in his Junior year at college, his mother wrote to him: "You ask me my son, what your pa thinks of religion or what his feelings are, I do not know, I am sure that he has great reverence for God and religion but my great trouble is that he does not come out before the world & accept the offers of mercy, I often wish to talk with him on the subject but feel so deeply my inability & am so sensible of my own leanness & inconsistency as a Christian that I shrink from the attempt." Inconsistent she may have been, but she saw to it that her children regularly attended Sunday School. At the age of twelve, at a Sunday School picnic of the Protestant churches, Sidney delivered the address for the Presbyterian Sunday School (VII, 16; Starke, 12).

His mother taught him music. Secular education was more difficult to come by. He attended private classes organized by various teachers, but the nearest to a regular school was the Bibb County Academy, which closed in 1854. Yet some of his instruction must have been excellent, for in January 1857, when he was examined for entrance into Oglethorpe College, he was admitted into the Sophomore Class (VII, 4).

Although he cared little for team sports, he enjoyed imaginative games. Aubrey Starke (13) has described one which Lanier probably invented: "He and Charles Wiley would play they were cotton dealers and take turns in being buyer and seller. The warehouses were tunneled out of the red clay sides of a deep gulley that ran alongside of the main highway leading to the business section of the town. Most of the cotton that entered Macon passed over this road, and the boys would jump out of the ditch and grab handfuls of fresh cotton off the wagons and store it in their 'warehouses'. Hickory nuts served as money, though sometimes—when raids of another sort were successful—they used pins. The cotton was weighed carefully on the simplest of scales, in the palms of the boys' hands."

The writers most directly influential on him in his early youth were Lord Byron and the medieval chroniclers of chivalry, especially Froissart and Malory. He wrote poems that his brother Clifford remembered as melancholy and Byronic. The legends of old days led him to organize a military company of about fifty boys, with bows and arrows substituted for guns. Captain Lanier drilled the Macon Archers so well that on patriotic holidays the company was allowed to march with the adult, war-tested Macon Volunteers and Floyd Rifles.

Yet what Lanier remembered with most pleasure in

later life were the family evenings at home, with the singing of hymns, old ballads and love songs accompanied by
his mother, and with the reading aloud by his father of
such favorite authors as Scott and Wordsworth and
Tennyson. Above all, he remembered the solitary rambles
through the woods and along the banks of the Ocmulgee
River, sensing even then an unusual personal rapport
with nature as he day-dreamed, or attempted to recapture
the sound of birdcalls on his flute.

Because of his mother's insistence, Sidney entered the
staunchly Presbyterian Oglethorpe College at Midway,
two miles from the state capital at Milledgeville, in January 1857. Although it seems he preferred the University
of Georgia or his father's alma mater, the Methodist
Randolph-Macon in Virginia, no complaint survives in
the extant letters. That he was unhappy and in poor
health is clear enough. He might be able to "do" forty-
five lines of Horace in fifteen minutes, as he boasted to his
father, but he stood only midway in his class, and his
conscience so hurt him, when he discovered that from
small borrowings he owed a classmate fifteen dollars, that
he wrote to his father, "I have sinned" (VII, 5–7). Apparently his main pleasure was in belonging to the
Thalian Literary Society and in playing the flute to those
students who would listen. Some of them later com-
mented that when playing he would seem to go into a
trance, oblivious of everything except the music.

His sinfulness may have bothered Lanier, but it went
unobserved by his fellow-students. Those who have left
records have unanimously testified that his conduct and
his speech were above reproach.

His second year started off uphappily when Lanier—by
that time continually in and out of love—was told by
Ophelia LeConte (sister of his roommate) that she could
have only a sisterly regard for him. Lanier fancied himself
as a cavalier, but an honorable one.

Because of his son's ill health and obsession with music, Robert Lanier withdrew Sidney from Oglethorpe. He spent the summer of 1858 at Montvale Springs; most of the fall and spring he worked at the post-office in Macon. His brother Clifford remembered that Sidney kept the supper table in laughter by his mimicry of Cracker dialect. It was from this, even more than from reading, that Lanier developed an interest in the dialect of the Negroes and the poor whites.

In the fall of 1859 Lanier re-entered Oglethorpe as a Senior. Probably just before that, he went on a ten-day camp-hunt in the Tennessee mountains and "killed two deer, running, about as near as I could estimate, as fast as the buckshot flew." He also boasted that on the hunt he had eaten a whole venison (VII, 21). Again in good health, Lanier prepared to study hard, although he complained of mental rustiness. Part of this contentment was undoubtedly traceable to the fact that his beloved younger brother Clifford had come to Oglethorpe and was rooming with him.

He could now appreciate the austere President, the Reverend Samuel K. Talmage, and the Professor of Mathematics Charles W. Lane, the "sunniest, sweetest Calvinist" on the faculty (Mims, 27–28). But the one who did most to influence Lanier's thinking was Professor James Woodrow, a man of thirty-one who had studied under Louis Agassiz at Harvard and had taken the degree of Doctor of Philosophy *summa cum laude* at Heidelberg. Woodrow was convinced that the scientific theory of evolution could be reconciled with Presbyterian theology; his own theory was more closely related to the environmental, organic theory of Lamarck than to the biological evolutionary theory of Darwin. Lanier could and did accept this, but he could never bring himself to believe in the naturalistic origin of species (X, 205).

Woodrow was also interested in German idealistic phi-

losophy and literature. Professor and scholar took long
walks together, discussing the ideas of Hegel and the poetry of Heine and Herder. About this time Lanier came
under the spell of Thomas Carlyle, and through him the
German romantic writers, especially Richter and Novalis.
Woodrow encouraged Lanier to learn German and
French, superintending his study of these languages (VII,
29).

At the end of the year, Sidney had the highest average
in his class. But the runner-up was so close that the Faculty appointed two valedictorians, with Lanier giving the
first address on the subject "The Philosophy of History."
At the same time, through the intercession of Professor
Woodrow, he was offered and accepted an appointment as
Tutor in the College at a salary of $550.00 a year.

The appointment pleased everybody in the family. Although Robert Lanier greatly enjoyed music and poetry,
he had felt compelled to point out that these were precarious ways of making a living. Sidney himself was uncer-
tain. In his diary he tried to assess what he wanted to do:
"The point which I wish to settle is merely by what
method shall I ascertain what I am fit for as preliminary
to ascertaining God's will with reference to me; or what
my inclinations are, as preliminary to ascertaining what
my capacities are—that is, what I am fit for. I am more
than all perplexed by this fact: that the prime inclination
—that is, natural bent (which I have checked, though) of
my nature is to music, and for that I have the greatest
talent; indeed, not boasting, for God gave it me, I have an
extraordinary musical talent, and feel it within me plainly
that I could rise as high as any composer. But I cannot
believe that I was intended for a musician, because it
seems so small a business in comparison with other things
which, it seems to me, I might do. Question here: 'What

is the province of music in the economy of the world?' "
(Mims, 38–39; *Poems*, xiv).

He spent the summer at Montvale Springs, fishing with
his father at the base of Chilhowee Mountain and taking
long rides on horseback (then and throughout the rest of
his life his favorite form of exercise), alone or in the company of friends. That summer he wrote a number of
rather conventional poems, some of which have survived,
and apparently made extensive notes for the first section
of his post-war novel, *Tiger-Lilies*.

When he returned to Oglethorpe, he had arrived at a
workable compromise. Instead of studying law as his
father wished, or becoming a professional musician and
composer, he would go to Heidelberg, take a doctorate,
and in the process qualify himself to teach literature in a
college or university. This decision his father accepted
with equanimity. James Woodrow was enthusiastic. The
long walks continued, but added to them were longer
buggy rides with Sidney accompanying the older man
when he preached at churches in the vicinity. With justice, Lanier later described Woodrow as "the strongest
and most valuable stimulus of his youth" (*Poems*, xiii).

Clifford Lanier remained his closest young companion.
But Sidney's position set him somewhat apart from the
students, though he noted wryly, with his incessant love of
punning, that because of his flute-playing his title of tutor
had been corrupted to that of tooter. Since he was no
longer a student, Sidney moved from Thalian Hall to a
nearby boarding house. In the adjoining room was Milton
H. Northrup, only a year older, a native of New York,
graduate of Hamilton College, and Principal of the
Oglethorpe Academy for Boys. Together they serenaded
young ladies, walked in the woods, talked about books
and ideas, and played chess badly. Northrup was a Demo-

crat, but he believed in the Union, and he tempered Sidney's secessionist tendencies at a time when Robert and Clifford Lanier were becoming hot-headed advocates of forming a new nation. Clifford joined an Oglethorpe military company, but Sidney did not.

Nonetheless, the emotional tension became increasingly hard to resist. On January 19, 1861, the state legislature in Milledgeville voted that Georgia secede. In April, the Macon Volunteers and the Floyd Rifles left for Virginia. On May 1 a Confederate flag was presented with elaborate ceremonies to the Oglethorpe "University Guards"; in what is perhaps his first work to be published, Sidney described the presentation in the Macon *Daily Telegraph,* May 15, 1861. Robert Lanier liked all of it except the pseudonym Cacoethes Scrib, which seemed to him classical claptrap. At some time during this period, the plan for graduate study in Germany went by the board. Lanier later admitted, ruefully, that he had become convinced of his ability to whip any five Yankees. Acting on this conviction, he enlisted in the Macon Volunteers early in July and soon afterward was on his way to Virginia (V, 197–99; VII, 41).

Lanier's company was stationed just outside Norfolk, at Sewall's Point. They drilled frequently; otherwise, their military duty was to guard the beach. There was as yet no hint of the grimness of war. The food was good; furloughs in Norfolk were frequent; when no furloughs were forthcoming, the soldiers, including Lanier, would change into civilian clothes in a cemetery vault where these were kept, and go through the cemetery into the city. The one unpleasantness was marsh agues "that played dice with our bones, and blue-mass pills that played the deuce with our livers" (VII, 226).

Lanier was under light rifle and artillery fire occasionally, but his most exciting early experience was witnessing the victory of the Confederate *Merrimac* (or *Virginia*) over the *Monitor*. He had written home earlier that she was "the ugliest Monster imaginable," but her victory stimulated Sidney to give five dollars toward the construction of more of these ironclad monsters (VII, 52, 55).

The Company was ordered in April 1862 to Wilmington, North Carolina, to help build Fort Fisher. Lanier noted that the main change was in the style of fever, to the "dry shakes of the sand-hills." He carried his flute everywhere with him in his haversack, and other men later recalled hearing some remarkably fine playing. The soldiers expected to be attacked near Goldsboro by General Burnside's army, but they were not. After a few weeks the Macon Volunteers returned to Virginia, to Drewry's Bluff on the James River between Richmond and Petersburg. About this time Clifford joined his older brother. According to tradition, Sidney steadily refused offers of promotion so that the two would not be separated. Virginia Hankins remembered them as "inseparable; slender, grey-eyed youths, full of enthusiasm, Clifford grave and quiet, Sidney, the elder, playful with a dainty mirthfulness."

His real baptism of fire, his first experience of the horrors of war, came in the "famous seven days battles around Richmond," June 26–July 2, 1862. Just before the battle of Malvern Hill on July 1, his Company marched all night over muddy roads in a drenching rain. It is possible that he was wounded here or later at Chancellorsville, for in 1874 thanking Logan E. Bleckley for encouraging words about his poetry, he wrote: "Did you ever lie, for a whole day, after being wounded,—and then have water brought you? If so, you will know how your words came to me." It is probable, however, that this was based on observation rather than personal experience, and that the question was meant to be rhetorical (VII, 226; IX, 98).

After the battles, Sidney and Clifford obtained transfers

to the Mounted Signal Corps. As they were expert horse-
men, they were in Major James Milligan's battalion but
attached to the staff of Major-General S. G. French. Their
duties were sometimes dangerous but rarely onerous.
They were supposed to keep marauding expeditions from
landing Federal gunboats, and to report any significant
movement of troops or vessels. The General and the Major loved music, and General French has recorded that
Sidney spent many evenings in his quarters. One evening
an impromptu group of troubadours serenaded in Petersburg; it consisted of one General, six Captains, one Lieu-
tenant, and four privates.

In his free time in Petersburg, Lanier continued his
study of German, and translated a few German poems
into English. He also composed and arranged a small
amount of music. But Sidney was frequently ill; apparently this was the beginning of the tuberculosis that
troubled him the rest of his life. And the war grew steadily more grim. On one march he half-carried his exhausted brother for miles; on another, when there were
no horses or mules available, he and a friend harnessed
themselves to a small wagon and pulled food and supplies
to the camp (VII, 64; *Poems,* xv–xvi).

In the spring of 1863, Sidney and Clifford were granted
furloughs and returned to Macon. Sidney's free time was
given to a double-barreled flirtation. For some years he
had enjoyed playing flute and piano duets with Augusta
(Gussie) Lamar, or accompanying her singing on the
piano. At her home he met his future wife, Mary Day,
tall, delicately beautiful, and a good pianist. His atten-
tions were so markedly ardent that when he left Macon in
April each girl was convinced that Sidney was in love with
her. In some of the most embarrassing letters ever published, Lanier continued this dual courtship for several
years; soon he made it a triple one. It never occurred to

him that he was not acting morally and honorably; rather, when he wrote a letter he abandoned himself completely to the luxury of sentiment and mood, however impermanent these might be. Gussie Lamar praised these epistles highly.

Robert Lanier found his son's letters not to his taste: "Letters however graceful which consist of mere emanations *from* the mind are never so interesting as those which are made up of *actualities* . . . put in plenty of facts, circumstances, & things pertaining to actual life as you see them or as they affect you." He particularly cautioned his impressionable son that in letters to young ladies he should avoid "too high colorings, exaggerations, false or perverted views of life's realities & the like." Sidney was temperamentally incapable of taking this wise advice. After a short description of a day's fighting to Mary Day, he added contemptuously, "that's more space than I ever devoted to mere news, in any letter of mine, before," and proceeded through many more pages to elaborate on his feelings about flowers, literature, and love. To his father he protested that "To Mary Day, I write precisely as I think and feel" (VII, 92n., 97–98, 79, 100).

The two-day battle of Chancellorsville rudely jerked him back to reality. Sidney's detachment had mainly a covering part in the action, but Clifford has graphically described the horror of artillery fire and a friend wrote later that Sidney, in rags, would not at first take a clean new shirt from a dead Federal soldier; conquering his squeamishness, he returned to find that some one else had not been delayed by like scruples. The death of Stonewall Jackson inspired one of his few war poems, but in later life he did not like to remember or to talk about the battles in which he had taken part (I, 156, 369).

Soon after, his signal detachment was ordered to scout near the mouth of the James River, opposite Newport

News, and transmit any information about army or navy
movements by a secret signal line to Petersburg. Normally
the detachment numbered only eighteen. The work was
dangerous at times, but Lanier never lacked physical
courage. There were compensations enough: "Our life,
during this period was as full of romance as heart could
desire. We had a flute and a guitar, good horses, a beautiful country, splendid residences inhabited by friends who
loved us, and plenty of hair-breadth 'scapes from the rov-
ing bands of Federals who were continually visiting that
debatable land. I look back on that as the most delicious
period of my life, in many respects: Cliff and I never cease
[June 1866] to talk of the beautiful women, the sere-
nades, the moon-light dashes on the beach of fair Bur-
well's Bay (just above Hampton Roads), and the spirited
brushes of our little force with the enemy" (VII,
226–27).

Here he met Virginia (Ginna) Hankins. John Hankins
owned and lived in Bacon's Castle, so named because it
had been fortified by Nathaniel Bacon in the rebellion of
1676. One night a group of young Confederates, including the Laniers, left a note tied to her front door with a
guitar string: "Did *all* that mortal men *could* to serenade
you—failure owing entirely to 'inclemency of the
weather.'—Field Corps" (Starke, 51–52). The soldiers
were invited back, and the Laniers quickly became close
friends of the family. Here, breaking the monotony of
camp fare, they enjoyed such luxuries as hot biscuits, Virginia ham, eggs, chickens, and, when they spent the night,
mint-juleps served before they were out of bed. But for
Sidney the main attraction was witty, handsome Ginna.
He fell in love with her, and immediately after the war
proposed to her at least once. He took occasion to initiate
her into the "beauties of Mrs. Browning and Robert B.,
together with Carlyle and Novalis" (Starke, 56). With

her encouragement and inspiration, he returned to writing.

Four of his poetic tributes to her, rather conventional love poems, have survived, and two translations from German. But his main literary pre-occupation was with the novel published later as *Tiger-Lilies* (1867); according to his letters, he did not actually start writing until 1863, although it seems likely that he had made some rough drafts in the summer of 1860 at Montvale Springs—the time and locale of the first part.

There were pleasant interludes in the grimly dangerous business of war. Early one morning some 300 Federal soldiers disembarked at Fay's Point in an attempt to capture the eighteen Confederate scouts and thus break up the sending of messages to headquarters. The battle lasted all day, but the invaders got only one mile from their transport, and that night withdrew. Lanier's detachment was commended in orders, but they lost their extra clothes, cots, cooking utensils and a dozen books, including Hugo's *Les Miserables*, Elizabeth Browning's *Aurora Leigh*, a volume of poems by Coleridge, Shelley, and Keats, and one by Heine. Because Lanier always carried his flute in his haversack, it was saved. He requested his father to send him editions of the poetry of Uhland, Lessing, Schelling, and Tieck, and told him: "Gradually I find that my whole soul is merging into this business of writing, and especially of writing poetry" (VII, 136–37).

In August of 1864, Sidney and Clifford were ordered to Wilmington, North Carolina, to act as signal officers on blockade runners. There were many delays, until on November 2 Sidney's ship ran the blockade successfully. But fourteen hours later it was captured. The British officers and sailors were released, but Lanier was held prisoner. He was sent in turn to Norfolk, to Fortress Monroe, to Camp Hamilton, and to Point Lookout, Maryland. He

carried his flute, hidden in his sleeve, with him throughout his months in prison.

His closest friend at Point Lookout was John Banister
Tabb, later a Catholic Priest and a distinguished poet.
Tabb sang to Lanier's accompaniment, and they talked at
length about poetry and music. Otherwise the prison was
a "hell-hole," as Tabb later described it, so bad that the
gentle priest could never forgive his enemies. The officer
in charge of prisoners Tabb denounced as an "unprinci-
pled, infamous character. The tents were leaky, the floors
the wet ground, and no fires were allowed. A Federal sur-
geon reported that the rations were inadequate and often
spoiled, and the water so bad that there was constant
diarrhoea, dysentery, and typhoid fever" (F. A. Litz,
Father Tabb, 22). Men died at the rate of fifteen to
twenty a day. Although Lanier glossed over the horrors of
prison life in *Tiger-Lilies,* he could not ignore them.

As Lanier wrote in *Florida,* tuberculosis ran in the
family; in his case, it "had everything in its favor at the
start—the prestige of inheritance on both sides." His lung
trouble increased gravely and by late February 1865
(after four months imprisonment), he was so ill that with
the aid of a little judicious bribery he was smuggled out
of prison, and on a river boat was nursed by an old friend.
But the slow, hard trip from Virginia to Macon, much of
it made on foot, so exhausted him that "losing the stimulus which had kept me going so long, I fell dangerously ill
and remained so for three months—delirious part of the
time" (VII, 227). In truth, Lanier never recovered from
this illness.

After a lengthy convalescence in the spring and summer
of 1865, he accepted a position as tutor of the five children of Mr. and Mrs. Thomas Fulton at Scott's Mill Plantation, nine miles from Macon. Work seemed a necessity,
even for a sick man. Although his grandfather still owned

the Exchange Hotel in Montgomery and Clifford had gone there as a clerk, the Montvale Springs property had been lost. His father's law practice had to be started anew. As an economy measure, the Laniers boarded at Wesleyan College. On May 22, 1865, Sidney's mother died. This was a period that with justice Sidney could describe with the accurately somber phrase, "Raven Days." Even the tutorial appointment proved deceptive, as Mrs. Fulton invited the children of neighboring planters to attend what had become a school. On September 30, 1865, Sidney wrote to Clifford that "I have little leisure; not a spare moment in the day-time, having to hear some Thirty classes every day—Consequently I have to do all my writing at night, and my failing health prevents me from sitting up late— It almost maddens me to be confined to the horrible monotony of Tare and Tret (it ought to be called Swear and Fret!), and B-a-k-e-r, Baker, when my brain is fairly teeming with beautiful things, at least, things that seem beautiful to me—" (VII, 200).

He found his major solace in music, especially with his old friend and musical companion, Gussie Lamar. Musicales were frequent. Sidney wrote an accompaniment for Tennyson's "Song of Elaine," in *Idylls of the King,* and some other musical pieces now apparently lost, but his major free time, socially, was devoted to Gussie, to such an extent that Virginia Hankins assumed they were to be married. Yet he continued to write ardent letters to Mary Day, even though she considered herself engaged to another man. When Gussie announced her plans to wed an older, wealthy man, Sidney wrote for her two poems: "The Wedding" seems to be an expression of personal grief, although it may be simply an expression of what Lanier felt was called for by the occasion; "The Wedding-Hymn" indicates that he had reconciled himself to whatever personal loss might be involved. In fact, about the same time he was writing for Mary Day "The Tournament: Joust First"—although later he used it in "Psalm of the West," an allegory of the Civil War.

These poems were a minor part of his writing; by September 1 he had completed three more chapters of *Tiger-Lilies;* by the 30th, another chapter, and a poem, "The Dying Words of Jackson"—probably the best of his war poems. War as he had known it had a modicum of chivalrous glamor; reconstruction did not. Years later he wrote in "Retrospects and Prospects" that the laws passed by Congress had caused "such a mass of crime and hatred and bitterness as even the four terrible years of war entirely failed to bring about."

This attempt to live a daily life on the plantation and a nightly life (though an innocent one) in Macon soon caught up with him. On his doctor's orders, in mid-October 1865, he gave up his tutorial position for a month, to go with his grandfather and uncle to Point Clear, Alabama, on Mobile Bay. When a regimen of simple living, horseback riding, and outdoor life brought a temporary respite, Sidney joined Clifford as a clerk in the Exchange Hotel, Montgomery. The work was not arduous. Each brother was busily engaged in writing a war novel: Clifford's, *Thorn-Fruit,* and Sidney's, *Tiger-Lilies* (both published in 1867). Probably this leisure time caused Sidney to refuse to return to the more lucrative job of tutoring (VII, 211).

There were a few bright spots. The New York *Round Table* accepted and published (though anonymously) at least two of his translations from German poets, and one original poem. The Reverend W. J. Scott of Atlanta, editor of *Scott's Monthly,* registered at the hotel; Sidney introduced himself, and Scott accepted a "prose article entitled 'Three Waterfalls', which struck me as being a masterpiece of wit and humor." These oases were few and far between. He was justified in writing to Northrup that there was "not enough attrition of mind on mind," and, much later, to Bayard Taylor that "with us of the younger generation of the South, since the war, pretty much the whole of life has been merely not dying." This is given added poignancy when one remembers that in July 1866, he became so desperately ill that he wrote to Northrup "no bone in me but aches, no nerve but tingles when I cough, shaken by that old bronchitis I caught in your inhospitable Point Lookout prison." When Lanier partially recovered, he abandoned his clerkship and went to New York to arrange for the publication of his novel, or, as he phrased it, with "bloody literary designs on some hapless publisher" (VII, 227–29, 234, 278).

The visit could hardly be termed a success, either from the literary or financial point of view. *The Round Table* published two more of his poems, signed with his name, but he was forced to subsidize (with the help of a Northern kinsman) the publication of his novel. Reluctantly he returned to work at the Exchange Hotel. But he found some consolation in becoming the organist at the Presbyterian Church.

His love affairs remained tangled. An Alabama girl, Anna Howard, was convinced that Sidney had proposed to her; when at his request Clifford interceded with her, he reported that she "is in a condition indescribable, wishes she were dead, vows vengeance on Sid, statelily calls him Mr. Lanier—when she does not speak of him as her ruin —and—and, and is preparing to wed a Mr. Metcalf." Clifford's mediation was effective, for on July 12, 1867, Sidney wrote that "Anna has written me a noble letter." Four days later, he proposed by letter to Virginia Hankins. She temporized, mainly on the ground that she could not leave her motherless young brothers and sisters. In less than a month, the impatient Sidney was engaged to

Mary Day. To hasten the wedding, he applied for and received the position of Principal of the Prattville, Alabama, Academy (VII, 297, 300, 301, 306, 309, 313).

In late September, Lanier rented a small house, hired two servants, and began teaching. But he and Mary were not married until December 19, 1867, partly because of Mary's illness with malaria. It was in fact the marriage of two semi-invalids. Yet except for nagging poverty and sickness which enforced frequent separations, the marriage was an idyllically happy one.

After a brief honeymoon in Macon, they returned to Prattville. Sickness was not long in striking. On January 17, 1868, he woke up with his mouth full of blood, and the hemorrhage from the lungs continued for half an hour. Yet he felt obliged to continue teaching, which he found increasingly onerous. Moreover, because of straitened economic times and the rigorous harshness of Reconstruction, the school dropped from over eighty students to about fifty. Lanier was forced to let one teacher go, and soon another left voluntarily. With a weak voice and an impaired constitution, Lanier found the school so unmanageable that he resigned at the end of May (VII, 369).

Yet, amazingly, he continued to write: several good poems, mainly on Reconstruction themes; the beginning of a novel that was never completed; some short fiction and essays; and at least five musical compositions, although only one, "Little Ella" (1868), was published during his lifetime. He also tried, unsuccessfully, to secure a University Professorship. Perhaps with this in mind he planned during the summer vacation to "work on my essays; and on a course of study in German and in the latin works of Lucretius, whom I have long desired to study" (VII, 389).

In June they settled at Scott's Mill. Mary Day was irritated that news of her pregnancy was common knowledge;

Sidney considered going into the real estate business at Brunswick, where his father-in-law had extensive land holdings, and he made at least two trips there. Yet a certain amount of critical recognition made him hesitate. A young Forsyth, Georgia, newspaperman, Joel Chandler Harris, had praised both *Tiger-Lilies* and the poems in *The Round Table;* more heartening, an established Southern poet, Paul Hamilton Hayne, wrote him warm letters of appreciation (VII, 394–96). It was the first approbation Lanier had received from a well-known literary man. With this encouragement, he put together a small volume of essays (never published in that form) and began a long narrative poem of the fourteenth century insurrection of the Flemish peasants, "The Jacquerie." This was never completed. By the first of the year, he acknowledged to himself that he could not make a living by writing; he began to read law in the firm of his father and uncle, Lanier and Anderson, while acting as clerk to make the necessary minimal income. The first of four sons, Charles Day Lanier, was born in September 1868.

In July of 1869, he passed the bar examination and was admitted to practice law. But his letters that spring indicate that he was more interested in playing flute concerts and in his "devotion to letters" than he was in reading Blackstone or even in trying to promote, in New York City, a plan to establish a rolling-mill on Mr. Day's property (VII, 10). He was glad to escape from business negotiations to attend the opera. Even so, he had exerted himself too much. A lengthy illness that summer forced Lanier to postpone any legal work until late in the fall.

At this point, he seemed almost ready to abandon writing. He published only a few short poems; he stopped working on the novel; he turned only spasmodically to his long narrative poem. He made a few public addresses, one advising graduates of a woman's college to stay out of politics lest they become unfeminine, but these seem at best perfunctory demand performances. He gave several flute concerts, but he felt that essentially he was vegetating. From this half-hearted attempt at combining law and art he was roughly awakened in May 1870, by a "severe hemorrhage from the lungs." He went first with his family to Lookout Mountain, Tennessee, to recuperate; he enjoyed the scenery and the visitors, and he read aloud to a group of friends, including Jefferson Davis, one of Paul Hamilton Hayne's poems ("A Summer Mood") which he had just received. But his persistent cough and his physical weakness remained unabated (VIII, 75, 80–82, 94).

At his father's urging, he started for Minnesota, since that climate was regarded as favorable for consumptives, but in New York he decided that he could not "endure the coal-dust" from the engines or the hardships of the three-day trip. Instead, he began under a doctor's supervision a weight-lifting treatment, in two months progressing from 130 to 260 pounds. On September 30 the doctor optimistically but erroneously pronounced him cured, and Lanier hastened back to Macon to be with Mary Day before the birth of their second son, Sidney, Junior, on October 17. Almost immediately he was ill again, and in March 1871, he tried the sea air at Brunswick, Georgia. After a brief stay he felt improved enough to return to Macon, but the improvement was in fact temporary (VIII, 103, 121, 127, 130, 133, 139, 144).

One bright spot was his correspondence with Paul Hamilton Hayne, the only writer of any reputation that he knew—and him only through letters. Yet he did not hesitate to make both general and minute criticisms (VIII, 145–48, 174–76). Another bright spot was his family, to whom he was devoted. He was unable to work regularly; from time to time he suffered from hemorrhages; he was disturbed by the severities of Reconstruction, and perhaps most of all by the embarrassing fact that he was largely dependent for a living on his father and his brother. He was pleased that some of his poems and articles were published by Southern magazines, and that "Thar's More in the Man Than Thar Is in the Land" was frequently reprinted, but this limited recognition brought little fame and less remuneration (VIII, 143, 150n., 157).

After a brief period of recuperation in Marietta, Lanier made a business trip to New York—fruitless except for his enjoyment of music, and a resumption of his weight-lifting cure. But the raw autumn winds and rains soon forced him back to Macon, where he again attempted to earn a living by the resumption of his law practice (VIII, 181).

In less than a year, this effort had to be abandoned. When neither Alleghany Springs in Virginia nor Marietta brought more than a temporary alleviation quickly followed by a relapse, Lanier reluctantly agreed to try a winter in Texas. This meant an even more drastic separation from his family than the earlier ones, but he did not consider taking Mary Day and the children to an unsettled, turbulent country. He broke the trip by a pleasant visit with his brother Clifford in Montgomery, then went on by train to New Orleans, by ship to Galveston, and by train and stage-coach to San Antonio. He arrived there exhausted (VIII, 262–77).

It was his right lung that was most severely affected (he describes himself in *Florida* as "travelling as valet to his right lung—a service in which he had been engaged for some years"), and this in turn affected his right arm. Yet he wrote, however painfully, long letters to his wife and father which contain, as Edwin Mims wrote (p. 117), sketches of "characters and scenes—sketches that show at once his knowledge of human nature and his ability as a reporter." His family suggested that to conserve his strength he write a tri-weekly instead of a daily letter, but this proposal Lanier indignantly rejected: "I will have none of this tri-weekly business: I *will* continue to write thee daily." Moreover, as soon as the air and long horseback rides over the prairies had partially restored his strength, he embarked upon a series of journalistic articles on Texas, in an attempt to pay at least part of his expenses (his father and brother had urged the trip on him, and were prepared to look after Sidney and his family). But the articles did not repay the research and were a drag on his energy. They were competent but superficial hackwork. Apparently Lanier soon recognized this and turned to background reading for his long poem, "The Jacquerie" (VIII, 280, 291, 314, 325).

In San Antonio it was music that absorbed his artistic interest. He played the flute often, by himself and with an orchestra composed mainly of German musicians; here he wrote several of the musical pieces that later made up his scanty repertoire of original works. The first that pleased him was "Field-larks and Black-birds" (evidently somewhat revised later and the title shortened to "Blackbirds"). To judge from his letters, he played it more often than any other of his compositions; he wrote to his wife that it was a "most beautiful piece . . . wherein I have mirrored Mons. Field-lark's pretty eloquence so that I doubt he wd. know the difference betwixt the flute and his own voice." He was even prouder of *Danse des Moucherons* (sometimes called the Gnat Symphony, although Lanier preferred Midge-dance). Lanier wrote to Mary that "I think enough of it to let it go forward as Op. 1. . . . I have put the grave oaks, the quiet shade, the sudden sunlight, the fantastic, contrariwise and evershifting midge-movements, the sweet hills afar off, and *thee* with thy earnest wide eyes—all, in the piece, and thus I like it." These specific statements explain Dr. Mims's generalized and perceptive statement (p. 142) that "He saw music as he heard poetry." He attached a sentimental value to a composition written for his wife, "Longing," but the extant fragments indicate that it was no better than his love poems. One other work, "Wind-Song," deserves to be mentioned; he played it for Dr. Leopold Damrosch on October 29, 1874, but it may well have been written or begun in San Antonio; he wrote to his wife that "When I finished he came and shook my hand, and said it was done like an artist: and that he was greatly astonished and pleased with the poetry of the piece and the enthusiasm of its rendering" (VIII, 329–31, 335; IX, 32, 110).

In San Antonio he made his almost irrevocable break with any form of business life. It was not an easy decision. He was, in fact, not quite certain whether to devote his time and energy to writing or to music. Soon after his return to Georgia in March 1873, he wrote to Clifford that he intended to "get to New York and go at my true labor. For I will never be at rest until I so arrange my life as to get myself leisure to write some books that now burn in my heart: I *must* write them: it is the command of God." Yet in the same letter he wrote that his wife begged him to sell a silver service in order to buy a silver Boehm flute (for $240.00), and two days later he wrote to Paul Hamilton Hayne that "whatever turn I have for Art is purely musical; poetry being, with me, a mere tangent into which I shoot sometimes. I could play passably on several instruments before I could write legibly: and since, then, the very deepest of my life has been filled with music, which I have studied and cultivated far more than poetry" (VIII, 336, 344, 346, 347).

Other troublesome factors delayed him. The most personal and pressing was the approaching birth of his third

child, to which Mary Day looked forward with justifiable
dread, so that he did not dare to leave her (Henry Wys-
ham Lanier was born June 28, 1873). There was also ever-
present the need for money. Lanier tried vainly to sell a
coal-lot and to secure a contract for furnishing charcoal to
an iron furnace. When these attempts came to nothing, he
started with feverish optimism in September for New
York.

His letters, especially those to his wife, are high-hearted
if impractical. He stopped in Baltimore to play a diversity
of musical compositions privately with friends and publicly in amateur concerts; he met the scholarly editor William Hand Browne, who later published much of his
work in the *Southern Magazine;* he sufficiently impressed
Asger Hamerik, composer, and Director of the Peabody
Academy of Music, that Hamerik gave him a letter of
recommendation to Theodore Thomas, probably the out-
standing musical conductor of the time in this country.
But Thomas was on tour, with the result that in New
York Lanier repeated on a more extensive scale his expe-
riences in Baltimore. Living conditions were pleasant; he
roomed and took meals with an old friend, the journalist
Salem Dutcher; through relatives and friends, he had a
chance to play his own "Black-birds" and "Swamp-Robin"
for the musical critic of the New York *Times;* with various musical groups he played privately, in churches, and
on one occasion at a concert in Brooklyn (his performance was praised by several newspapers, but Lanier wrote
that "I only played for the fun of it."). There is no record
that he received any pay for these concerts, although
Lanier seems to have felt the praise sufficient compensation. More practically, realizing that he had only scant
training, he studied for some two months the technique of
flute-playing. But with Lanier music was essentially an
emotional rather than an intellectual experience; after an

early concert, Sidney wrote to Mary Day that "Music lifts me to a Heaven of Pain." In Hamerik's phrase, his response to music was "intuitive and spontaneous" (VIII, 401–19, 429).

Hamerik in Baltimore had offered him the position of *Flauto Primo* in the newly-formed Peabody Symphony Orchestra, at a salary of $120.00 a month. Lanier temporized, hoping to play with Theodore Thomas; when this failed to materialize, he accepted Hamerik's offer, although the salary had been cut in half, with slight extra pay for solo performances. The work, he noted, was light, and he should be able to augment the salary with some pupils: but like so many of Lanier's eager hopes this one came to nothing. This did not bother Mary Day too much: his wife recognized her uneconomical if not indeed extravagant housekeeping, and with considerable justice signed one letter "Thy *Costly* Luxury" (VIII, 304, 412).

He knew his father would disapprove, and on November 29 he attempted an elaborate justification:

> Why should I,—nay, how *can* I—, settle myself down to be a third-rate struggling lawyer for the balance of my little life,—as long as there is a certainty, almost absolute, that I can do some other things so much better? Several persons, from whose judgment in such matters there can be no appeal, have told me, for instance, that I am the greatest flute-player in the world: and several others, of equally authoritative judgment, have given me almost equal encouragement to work with my pen. (Of course, I protest against the necessity which makes me write such things, about myself:—I only do so, because I so appreciate the love and tenderness which prompt you to desire me with you, that I will make the fullest explanation possible of my course, out of reciprocal honor and respect for the motives which lead you to think differently from me.) My dear father, think how, for twenty years, through poverty, through pain, through weariness, through sickness, through the uncongenial at-

mospheres of a farcical college and of a bare army and
then of an exacting business-life, through all the discour-
agements of being born on the wrong side of Mason-and-
Dickson's line and of being wholly unacquainted with
literary people and literary ways,—I say, think how, in
spite of all these depressing circumstances and of a thousand more wh. I could enumerate, these two figures of
music and of poetry have steadily kept in my heart, so
that I could not banish them (VIII, 423–24).

This is an able if somewhat over-written defence. It is not
to be dismissed as the equivalent of special pleading, for
Lanier was becoming increasingly convinced that God revealed himself to man through the arts, especially music
and poetry, rather than through the church or through
theology. His own playing frequently brought on a trance-
like state of spiritual ecstasy in which he forgot entirely
the mundane world. According to Asger Hamerik, sincer-
ity and intensity of feeling more than compensated for a
sometimes faulty technique:

> His playing appealed alike to the musically learned and
> to the unlearned—for he would magnetize the listener:
> but the artist felt in his performance the superiority of
> the momentary living inspiration to all the rules and
> shifts of mere technical scholarship. His art was not only
> the art of art, but an art above art (*Poems,* xxxii).

Nonetheless, he frequently regretted his lack of formal
musical training and marvelled at his own temerity when,
"guiltless of instruction," he dared to join a professional
orchestra organized "expressly to play the most difficult
works of the great masters" (IX, 56).

The concert season over, Lanier turned again to the
writing of poetry—most notably "Corn," written when he
was with his family at Sunnyside in July 1874—and articles on music. In order to give the flute more prominence
in orchestras, he devised a new, longer instrument that
would have greater musical range.

In August he went to New York with several nebulous plans in mind: to become music critic on a Baltimore or New York newspaper; to secure a position as flutist in Theodore Thomas's Orchestra; to have several of his musical compositions published. He was tinkering with the idea that after magazine publication he would bring out "Corn" as a small illustrated book. He was goading A. L. Badger into experimenting with his new long flute, but Badger refused to produce it commercially because he thought it unmanageable. He began a translation of Wagner's *Rhein-Gold,* although he admitted that his knowledge of German was "but limited" (IX, 118–19). At the same time he was suffering enough with his right lung and arm that he occasionally "inflicted a left-hander" on his wife. Although he planned to make a living by poetry and music, he admitted that he was "without any definite plans as yet," and it may well be that this scattering of his weakened energy prevented any one of them from being brought to completion. Reluctantly giving up hope on these projects, he agreed in November to return as first flutist in the Peabody Symphony Orchestra, at a slight raise in salary from fifteen dollars a week to twenty (IX, 70–113).

There were a few bright spots. His poems were more readily accepted by magazine editors. A dialect poem written in collaboration with Clifford was accepted by J. G. Holland, editor of *Scribner's Monthly;* "Corn" brought him fifty dollars from *Lippincott's.* Even more important, such publications brought him the friendship of the Gibson Peacocks, and through them, later, of Bayard Taylor. From this time on, Lanier devoted more effort to writing and less to music, although he continued to wax ecstatic over his part in successful concerts.

He turned his restless attention to securing a chair in the Physics and Metaphysics of Music in the Peabody Institute, in Johns Hopkins, in Mercer, or in the newly-created New York College of Music. None of these academic positions materialized. It is not clear what qualifications he possessed, but for over two years he remained hopeful for a position that would allow him to divide his time, without pecuniary worries and with his family with him, "betwixt the music and the poetry."

He had not, however, abandoned the writing of poetry. In March 1875, the idea for a poem "took hold of me like a real James River Ague"; out of this came "The Symphony," published in *Lippincott's,* which gained him many new friends and admirers; more pertinently yet more disconcertingly, it brought him an offer from the Atlantic Coast Line to write a guidebook on Florida for railroad travellers. By his standards, the pay was good: $125.00 a month, plus hotel-bills and transportation expenses. But the idea of doing such a book was demeaning, though he was allowed a good bit of latitude: "I am to do Norfolk, Richmond, Petersburg, Wilmington, Raleigh, Charlotte, Columbia, Augusta, Charleston, Savannah, Jacksonville, St. Augustine, and Florida generally: I am to relate their histories, account their products, immortalize their great men, describe their topographies, and depict their points of interest . . . to get up a Guide-book which shall at once be a literary attraction and a statistical thesaurus. I owe all these honors to my Maecenas' having read "Corn'." However reluctantly, Lanier felt compelled to accept "the offer" (IX, 183).

The work took six months instead of the allotted three. Although Lanier realized that only a pot-boiler was wanted, he did a heavy amount of library reading and a relatively vast amount of travel (in fact, the record of his adult travels indicates that a robust man might well have succumbed; for a consumptive they would be unbelievable except that they are fully documented). Before he started for Florida, he went for a visit to the Peacocks in Philadelphia, there meeting the actress Charlotte Cushman, then to New York, and on to Boston, ostensibly to get an estimate of the cost of his book on Florida although this was not a part of his responsibility. Unless he was actively hemorrhaging, Lanier flatly refused to take care of himself. One account to his wife, not quite typical but not unusual, is illustrative: "I had a running day of it in New York: saw Foster & Parkman for a few minutes, talked with Mr. [J. F. D.] Lanier & Charles about Florida, (they have just returned from there) had a pleasant interview with Mr. Gilder (of *Scribner's Monthly*) and obtained permission for Miss Cushman to read the 'Power of Prayer', saw Hurd & Houghton about the Florida book, had a talk with the McDonald's, rushed over to Brooklyn and got hugged and kissed by Anna Mary and dined with the Ripleys . . . then back to 42nd street depôt where I took cars for Boston." A day later he returned to New York, and on the next to Baltimore (IX, 189–90).

After a brief period of rest with his family in Brunswick, Lanier went alone to Florida. Although not so rushed, the travel itself was fatiguing. He went first to Jacksonville, then to St. Augustine (which he found the most interesting city in Florida), then by boat up the Oklawaha River. Possibly the fresh impressions but more likely the romantic surroundings and the fact that he wrote them himself make these the best chapters in the book. When *Lippincott's* wanted advance articles immediately, he was forced to call on Mary Day for help. He could write only a few lines at a time; most of the book was dictated while they were traveling together and after they returned to Brunswick. But his travels were by no means over. In addition to visiting small towns in Florida, he had to go to Savannah, Augusta, Wilmington, to Macon on family affairs, back to Savannah and Brunswick,

Columbia, and Philadelphia. Here he discovered that his earlier attempts to arrange for the publication of the book had been futile: Lippincott & Company was to bring it out under a co-operative arrangement with the railroad, but it was necessary that he make brief trips to secure additional material, and that he be on hand to read proof and supervise the publication. He called himself a shuttlecock, and for once his tendency toward exaggeration seems an understatement. His drudgery was barely finished in time for the book to be published in early December (IX, 199–201, 219, 224, 226).

Not quite all his time was spent in work. At Bayard Taylor's invitation, he sat in Taylor's box for the Goethe Festival, met William Cullen Bryant, and was genuinely delighted with Taylor's "beautiful ode" on Goethe. He was pleased that good magazines continued to publish his poems and articles. But he suffered his greatest literary humiliation when he felt compelled to accept an offer from the *Lippincott* editor to write four articles on India, for $300.00. The editor made the offer in all innocence: he assumed from "Nirvâna" that Lanier was thoroughly familiar with the country. In fact, Lanier knew practically nothing about India, and his concept of Buddhism was erroneous; to palliate this he invented a person "Bhima Gandharva . . . only another name for Imagination. . . . I hit upon this expedient, after much tribulation and meditation, in order at once to be able to make something of a narrative that should avoid an arid encyclopedic treatment, and to be perfectly truthful." This was a weak apologia, and Lanier knew it; he was doing a piece of hackwork for the money involved, and he found the task irksome (IX, 249, 255, 279).

Perhaps one reason for his accepting the commission was that the editor, J. F. Kirk, asked him to write a Centennial poem for the magazine, and the "whole idea of the poem has come to me in a whirlwind of glory." This was exhilarating, but he continued to feel the need for a steady income; he asked Mr. Lippincott to create for him the job of Assistant-Editor of the magazine, to be told that it was doing badly and might be discontinued. Lanier took this blow in stride, and went on to Boston to visit with the dying Charlotte Cushman. What might have been a calming, solicitous trip was disturbed by a review of *Florida* in the *Nation;* the reviewer objected to his "rhetorical-poetical foible of seeing 'God in everything.'" The criticism was documented, but the outraged Lanier objected vehemently to the use of the word *foible* (IX, 265, 266). Although by this time he had broken with orthodox Christianity, he believed (and continued to believe) in the immanence of God.

Although in Boston he spent most of his time with Miss Cushman, he worked in pleasant calls on Longfellow and Lowell (Taylor had given him letters of introduction). After a brief stay in Macon he returned late in November to Baltimore, taking his son Charles with him. He could not bear, he said, to be separated from all his family. He felt that the sight of his son's excitement at Christmas was adequate compensation for any inconveniences he had undergone.

Professionally, he was enormously pleased when, at the suggestion of Bayard Taylor, he was invited to write the words of the Centennial Cantata, with music by Dudley Buck. This lyric took practically all of his creative thought during the month of January 1876, for he wanted to make it "as simple and as candid as a melody of Beethoven's." When the words without the music were published, the lyric brought forth almost poisonous attacks in the Northern newspapers and was vehemently defended (mainly on sectional partisanship) by the South. Lanier was troubled, but he consoled himself with the knowledge

that the composer, Dudley Buck, and the leader of the
Orchestra, Theodore Thomas, admired the work perceptively. The poem was written to be sung. In one respect
Lanier's judgment was confirmed: when sung by a chorus
of 800 voices accompanied by an orchestra of 150 musicians, the ensemble skillfully conducted by Thomas, it was
so enthusiastically received that Bayard Taylor wrote to
the New York *Tribune* that the "effect upon the audience
could not be mistaken." President Gilman thought a
"noble conception had been nobly rendered. . . . Lanier
had triumphed." The sore festered. Lanier prepared an
indignant refutation, but Taylor persuaded the *Tribune*
to publish both poem and music, with an explanatory
introduction by Taylor. In a calmer moment, Sidney
wrote to Clifford that the "commotion about the Cantata
had not been unfavorable on the whole to my personal
interests" (IX, 288, 292–312, 352–55, 363, 374–75).

Almost immediately, Lanier started his long Centennial
Ode, "Psalm of the West." He took time from this and
other work to attend the funeral of his friend Charlotte
Cushman; as usual, he tried to do too much and had to
recuperate for several days after he returned to Baltimore,
although he found energy enough to write a brief poem
in her honor. Except for his regular concerts, Lanier hus-
banded his energy to work on the Ode. He announced it
as completed on April 4, although he later made significant changes. It was the longest poem he wrote, three
times as long as "The Symphony." With this out of the
way, he joyfully accepted a proposal by her long-time
companion, Emma Stebbins, that they collaborate on a
biography of Charlotte Cushman. It would be a "noble
project" and pay him well, but only preliminary planning
on it was ever done (IX, 348, 350–52, 371–72, 384–85,
390).

With this project in suspense, Lanier turned to minor

projects, including an article on "The Physics of Music" (it was not published until after his death). But he continued to fret over what seemed to him savage and untruthful reviews, even after he moved his family to West Chester, Pennsylvania, for the summer, and he vented his feelings in a long letter to the *Tribune*. Soon afterward he collapsed, and on July 19 wrote Taylor "I'm just crawling back into some sort of shambling activity after a very depressing illness." To his father he admitted that he found it "difficult, while ill and unable to work, to raise money for daily expenses" (IX, 387, 391, 404).

He attempted unsuccessfully to secure a Professorship of Poetry and Music at Johns Hopkins; he was pleased that Lippincott had brought out a volume of his poems, but discontented with it on two counts: since it included only those poems that had appeared in the magazine, it did not give a sufficient representation of his work, and he had sold the book as well as the magazine copyright of the longer poems. He planned to return to the Peabody Orchestra, but early in December 1876, his doctor warned him that a winter in Baltimore would cause his death, although he declared valiantly that nothing "could induce me to die before I've written and published my fine additional volumes of poetry." Later that month Sidney and his wife went to Tampa, Florida. There, forbidden to write, he rebelled "against tyranny" and sent many letters to family and friends, and continued to write poems. Although his own health improved, Mary suffered from "malarial influences," and in April they moved to Brunswick. While in Tampa he read carefully for the first time the work of Emerson, "who gives me immeasurable delight because he does not propound to me disagreeable systems and hideous creeds." Emerson lent support to Lanier's increasing pantheism (IX, 411, 417, 426, 431, 440, 446).

On the insistence of his father, he unwillingly consented to apply for a government position, and went north to confer halfheartedly with federal officials. This, he thought, demeaned his dignity; when he was offered a minor diplomatic post in China, he peremptorily turned it down. He preferred to wait for a possible position in the State or Treasury departments. He took his family to Chadd's Ford, Pennsylvania, for the summer.

Probably the brightest incident was a renewal through correspondence of his war-time friendship with John Banister Tabb. Lanier had been told in Baltimore that Tabb was dead; he was in fact studying for the Roman Catholic priesthood in St. Charles College, Maryland, and writing the brief mystical poems that won him a minor degree of fame. Because of Tabb's excessive shyness, they saw each other only a few times, but they corresponded until Lanier's death, with Tabb frequently enclosing poems for suggestions and criticism. Lanier objected to some of Tabb's approximate rhymes: he desired flexibility in rhythm, but not in rhyme (IX, 465–66, 469–70, 472–75, 505–07).

In the autumn he returned to Baltimore, this time taking his entire family with him. Their four rooms were near the Johns Hopkins University, the Peabody Institute, and the Academy of Music; their meals were sent up from the restaurant in the basement. Lanier found time to give Richard Malcolm Johnston kindly suggestions on one of his Dukesborough Tales and, on a trip to New York, to place it with *Scribner's*. He was less successful in his attempt to get for himself lucrative magazine commissions or a contract to write a book on Georgia similar to his *Florida*. But "running about too much in New York" brought on a severe hemorrhage that prostrated him for two weeks. It was a sickly household: the boys had "wretched colds" and Mary a recurrence of her catarrhal troubles. Discontented with the apartment, Lanier rented a nine-room house for a year. When his father doubted the wisdom of this, Sidney answered over-optimistically: "How I wish I could inspire you with my own confidence in my future, financially and otherwise." They moved a few days before Christmas, and Lanier wrote ecstatically of the joys of having Christmas with his family in their new home. He also hired a "colored gentlewoman" to do the cooking and cleaning. He was, in fact, in "a state of supreme content with our new home." But the excitement, pleasurable though it might be, brought on "a raging fever" that once again put him to bed (IX, 503, 509; X, 3–7).

A few nights later he performed with the Peabody Symphony Orchestra. But he felt an "unconquerable longing to stop all work for a few months except the study of Botany, French, and German, and the completion of a long poem ["The Jacquerie"] which I have been meditating," and he tried to borrow money against a tract of Georgia timber-land which he had inherited. Apparently for the first time, he read Whitman's *Leaves of Grass* and found it "a real refreshment to me—like rude salt spray in your face." However, he objected to Whitman's "fundamental error that a thing is good because it is natural," and noted there was a "world-wide difference between my own conceptions of art and its author's" (X, 18, 40).

A long-time friend, Mrs. Edgeworth Byrd, invited Lanier to give a series of eight lectures on the Elizabethan poets, for a stipend of $100.00. Lanier accepted, but limited the topic to the sonnets. He also taught one class a day at R. M. Johnston's Penn Lucy School for girls. He did not enjoy the teaching, but thought the lectures might lead to similar engagements. He began a careful study of the early English poets, but he did not begrudge the labor—in fact, he found it congenial. More immediately, the Peabody Orchestra gave him a complimentary concert, which netted him $164.00. This windfall helped, but it was not enough. Yet, characteristically, he took time off to do research on the Lanier family for a cousin, J. F. D. Lanier, and proved to his own satisfaction (though not to many genealogists) that he was descended from the Nicholas Laniers, father and son, who had been prominent musicians in Elizabethan and Jacobean days (X, 26, 28, 32–33, 37–38).

The Peabody Institute asked him to give a series of fifty lectures, November through April, on English poetry through Shakspere. He planned to devote the entire summer to preparing them—a prospect which filled him with delight. In addition, he was working on several magazine articles on the Physics of Poetry, and, most important of all, he wrote his first long poem, "The Marshes of Glynn." A few days later, he was proposing to Lippincott for almost immediate publication an anthology of English sonnets, from Surrey through Shakspere; and he had agreed to do for Scribner a redaction of Froissart's Chronicles, with "the uninteresting and objectionable parts expurgated, and accompanied by a historical and explanatory introduction, designed especially for boys" (X, 53, 62, 64, 66).

When *The Boy's Froissart,* elaborately illustrated, appeared in November 1879, it was so successful that Scribner planned a series to be called "The Boy's Library of Legend and Chivalry," with one volume edited by Lanier to be published each November. *The Boy's King Arthur* (1880) was equally successful, and at his death Lanier had completed work on *The Boy's Mabinogion* (1881) and *The Boy's Percy* (1882). These lesser works were not successful, but Lanier had also done some editing on *The Boy's Monstrelet* and *The Boy's Gesta Romanorum,* and on the Paston letters to begin a similar series for girls. Lanier was liberal with his excisions, but the Froissart and the Arthur remained popular for many years. Unfortunately Lanier, with his usual lack of financial acumen and his incessant need for money in hand, accepted $350.00 for each book, in lieu of royalties (X, 85, 89, 291, 301).

Volatile as always when feeling halfway well, Lanier proposed to deliver lectures in Washington and Philadelphia; since they were to be a systematic presentation of an announced subject, Lanier envisioned them as inaugurating throughout the country Schools for Grown People. Since only a few adults enrolled, the lecture series was dropped (X, 76–78, 86).

He was disappointed also in the anonymous publication of "The Marshes of Glynn" in *A Masque of Poets* (1878). If the contributors had read English poetry through Chaucer, they "could never be content to put forth these little diffuse prettinesses and dandy kickshaws of verse." But his feelings were mollified when Longfellow almost immediately praised the poem and asked permission to reprint it, with Lanier's name attached, in his projected anthology, *Poems of Places.* Lanier quickly gave the permission (X, 88, 95).

Even more exhilarating was a letter from President Gilman informing him that the Trustees of Johns Hopkins had unanimously voted to invite Lanier to become Lecturer in English Literature the next academic year, at a salary of $1,000. It was not a Professorship, but Lanier hoped to "make it the opening wedge towards my favorite chair" (of Music and Poetry). He not only began preparing the lectures, but he planned, and proposed to Scribner's, a series of textbooks; two of these *(The Science of English Verse* and an anthology, *From Caedmon to Chaucer)* he hoped to get published that year. He was also intent on publishing a second volume of his poems, and unsuccessfully negotiated with Lippincott to buy back the copyright of "The Symphony" and "Psalm of the West." When his plan for the projected books ran into outright rejections or discouraging delays, he proposed to Clifford that they start their own firm, Lanier Brothers. Wisely, Clifford refused to go into a business about which they knew practically nothing (X, 98–102, 113–14, 116, 120–21, 132, 142–43).

Recognizing that "Time is everything to me," he labored frantically on several books that summer, at Rockingham Mineral Springs in Virginia. Reluctantly he admitted that this was impossible, and concentrated on the book on verse. He studied and wrote from early morning until four in the afternoon; then with his two older sons he cantered on horseback on the mountain roads. When in mid-September he returned to Baltimore, he insisted on carrying the heavy manuscript himself.

Before he started back to work, he found it necessary to spend two weeks in bed. His schedule was enough to daunt anyone. In addition to his writing and editing, his Johns Hopkins lectures, and his Peabody Orchestra concerts, he had agreed to lecture (for $800) on English Literature at three private schools for girls. One consolation was that he seemed financially secure, for the first time since his marriage (X, 145, 147).

Although Scribner readily accepted *The Boy's King Arthur* (1880), the firm demanded a subsidy of $375 for the publication of *The Science of English Verse*. Grudgingly, since he had found it impractical to publish the book himself, Lanier accepted the offer. It appeared in late spring, 1880, for Lanier found the proofreading slow and onerous work. This task over, he prepared a synopsis of an Orchestral Handbook, and offered to prepare more courses for Johns Hopkins; the only one that materialized had at one time or another several titles: "From Aeschylus to George Eliot"; "A Study in the Development of Personality"; and in its published form after his death, *The English Novel* (1883). He was re-appointed Lecturer, at the same salary. This relieved a major worry, but by June he was once more exhausted and feverish. Even so, he attempted to persuade Scribner's to bring out a comparative study of Chaucer and Shakspere. Scribner was also pressing him for the complete text of *The Boy's King Arthur*, which Lanier sent on July 15, 1880. At that point his doctor "decisively ordered" him out; with his family and father-in-law he went to West Chester, Pennsylvania (X, 165–94, 208–16).

Lanier blamed this new illness on "the nervous strain of *waiting*. . . . I have had such a rush and storm of ideas demanding immediate expression, and have had to put aside such an enormous proportion of them in favor of small daily duties which physically limited me to a book or two a year, that I have been continually jarred and shaken with ever-recurrent shock and resistance." Especially he regretted that he had been forced to crush back poem after poem of which he had made memoranda, but had lacked time and energy to put his outline notes into completed poems (X, 220–21).

On August 14, 1880, his fourth son, Robert Sampson, was born. Lanier was delighted, and apparently unworried about the expense of providing for another child. Yet within a month he was again desperately ill, although he forced himself to complete the Introduction to his *King Arthur*. He requested President Gilman to postpone his University Lectures until early the next year, and gave up his other school engagements, but he went back to his work on *The Boy's Mabinogion,* and finished it in November. Also, with casual disregard for his health, he proposed to give a series of lectures on the English Satirists. Instead of added work, his doctors in December decreed that only tent life in a high altitude held out any chance for a cure. Lanier at first refused to leave Baltimore, and in fact gave some of the scheduled lectures. It was not until May, when he was offered $1500 to write on the summer resorts of the region by the Associated Railways of Virginia and the Carolinas, that Sidney consented to the plan—this at a time when to "dress in the morning completely exhausts me before my day is begun" (X, 253–64, 289, 304–07).

Although Lanier made some introductory researches, the writing of this book was never started. He completed *The Boy's Percy* and sent it to Scribner's; he accepted a reappointment as Lecturer at Johns Hopkins, writing that he was getting "stronger from day to day," though his wife realized that he was "almost in a collapse." He rallied sufficiently to write the magnificent lyric, "Ballad of Trees," and the feverishly uneven but occasionally beautiful poem, "Sunrise" (Starke overpraises it when he called it "a great poem, great as any in our American literature"). It was indeed a remarkable achievement for a dying man. He died on September 7, 1881, near Lynn, North Carolina, and was buried in Baltimore (X, 313–23; Starke, 411).

II   *The Poet*

SIDNEY LANIER hoped to become a major poet, and desired that his work be judged on that basis. Overpraise
of regional literature disgusted him. As early as 1869 he attacked the "insidious evil . . . of regarding our literature
as *Southern* literature, our poetry as *Southern* poetry, our
pictures as Southern [*sic*] pictures. I mean the habit of
glossing over the intrinsic defects of artistic productions by
appealing to the Southern sympathies of the artist's coun-
trymen" (V, 260). He was confident that his own work did
not need uncritical partiality. After the rejection of "Corn"
by *Scribner's* and the *Atlantic,* and after much agonized
introspection, he wrote to his wife "I *know,* through the
fieriest tests of life, that I am, in soul, and shall be, in life
and in utterance, a great poet" (IX, 109).

He did not achieve that goal. He never became even a
major American poet, in the sense that Poe and Whitman
and Dickinson are. There are valid, often tragic, reasons.
Throughout his adult life he suffered from tuberculosis to
an extent that almost every time he completed a major or
extended work he was incapacitated by severe hemorrhages of the lungs. His early death cut short work on

three projected volumes of verse. For these, he left numerous poem outlines that rarely got much beyond the note-taking stage. A third factor was the precarious state of his personal finances, ranging from downright poverty to, at best, an insufficient and unstable income. Poverty forced him into literary hackwork, sometimes good, as in his redactions for boys of Froissart and of Malory; sometimes respectable, as in the erratic but occasionally brilliant guide and travel book, *Florida;* sometimes degrading, as in the magazine sketches on India, a country which he had never seen. Yet even the best of these sapped energy from a man who had little vitality to spare.

Lanier himself was in part to blame. Although he recognized that a "great artist should have the sensibility and expressive genius of Schumann, the calm grandeur of Lee, and the human breadth of Shakspere," he could never attain mental or moral calmness and equanimity (X, 103). He had no sooner partially recovered from a tubercular attack than he was planning grandiose projects, many of which he was poorly equipped to carry out. His application for a fellowship in the newly-established Johns Hopkins University is almost unbelievable, for it was beyond the ability of a young, vigorous, well-trained man; in September 1877, Lanier was thirty-five years old, in poor health, and with a decidedly sketchy academic background: "My course of study would be: first, constant research in the physics of musical tone; second, several years devotion to the acquirement of a thoroughly scientific *general* view of Mineralogy, Botany and Comparative Anatomy; third, French and German Literature" (IX, 474). President Gilman would have none of what Lanier admitted "may seem a nondescript and even flighty process," although some justification can be found in his belief that good poetry could not be written in his time "unless that poetry and your soul behind it are informed and saturated with at least the largest final conceptions of current science." Even more disruptive and irrelevant was the plan, growing out of his lectures in Baltimore, to edit an extensive series of anthologies of English poetry and (when established publishers rejected the projects) to publish them himself, although he had little experience as an editor and none as a publisher. At the time when he most needed to husband his energies and concentrate on his major talent, Lanier was spreading himself dangerously thin.

Two other stumbling-blocks he threw in the way of the reader. One was his incessant moralizing and didacticism; it may be justifiable to believe, as Lanier firmly did, that in literature morality is more important than artistry, but it is irritatingly quite another thing to "forgive" writers like Homer, Socrates, Dante, and Shakspere (among many others: see "The Crystal") because they sometimes did not live up to his intransigent moral tone, or to dismiss Fielding and Smollett because their works seemed to him prurient. Too frequently Lanier lost all critical perspective, and this loss of perspective vitiates many of his own poems, as it does in "The Crystal." Less important is his fondness for archaic words and phraseology, his propensity in images to mix the concrete and the abstract, and his use of musical devices to such an extent that many readers consider his poems artificial and contrived.

These defects may be freely admitted, and some of them will be examined later, but there remains a residue of work that is excellent and germinal. In his major poems Lanier aimed at greatness of thought and expression. He recognized the possibility of failure, but the risk seemed worth taking. He wrote to Bayard Taylor about his younger contemporary poets that "I am struck with the circumstance that none of them even *attempt* anything great. The morbid fear of doing something wrong

or unpolished appears to have influenced their choice of
subjects. Hence the endless multiplication of those little
feeble magazine-lyrics which we all know; consisting of
one minute idea, each, which is put in the last line of the
fourth verse, the other three verses and three lines being
mere sawdust and surplusage." Even the greatest of writers
(Homer, Dante, Shakspere) had committed "enormous
artistic crimes," but their positive accomplishments far
over-shadowed their occasional lapses (IX, 413). Late in
life he expressed gratitude to Walt Whitman for

> such large and substantial thoughts uttered in a time
> when there are, as you say in another connection, so
> many "little plentiful mannikins skipping about in col-
> lars and tailed coats." Although I entirely disagree with
> you in all points connected with artistic form, and in so
> much of the outcome of your doctrine as is involved in
> those poetic exposures of the person which your pages so
> unreservedly make, yet I feel sure that I understand you
> therein, and my dissent in these particulars becomes a
> very insignificant consideration in the presence of that
> unbounded delight which I take in the bigness and brav-
> ery of all your ways and thoughts. It is not known to me
> where I can find another modern song at once so large
> and so naive: and the time needs to be told few things so
> much as the absolute personality of the person, the suffi-
> ciency of the man's manhood *to* the man, which you have
> propounded in such strong and beautiful rhythms (X, 40).

He believed also that "the artist shall put forth, humbly
and lovingly and without bitterness against any opposition, the very best and highest that is within him, utterly
regardless of contemporary criticism" (IX, 369). Yet, hu-
manly, he was troubled by what he regarded as mistaken
and unjust criticism. Later interpretations have not always improved the picture. Too often Lanier has been
praised or condemned for the wrong reasons, and the sane
commentaries of Aubrey Starke and Charles R. Anderson
have been glided over.

The extant poems written when he was at Oglethorpe College, few in number and deficient in quality, are of value mainly in revealing the great if transitory influence of Poe, Byron, and Coleridge, and the quieter but more enduring influence of his "dearest friend" Keats (I, 228). Sidney's brother Clifford remembered the college poems, many of them no doubt lost, as being *"Byronesque,* if not *Wertheresque,* at least tinged with gloominess" (Starke, 37). But the gloomy introspection of Byron and Poe was soon replaced by the bracing saneness of Tennyson and, mainly through his favorite essayist Carlyle, by the romantic sentimentalism of the German writers Richter and Novalis. These men had direct formative influence on Lanier's thoughts, and on his writing. Even more direct because it was personal was the influence of Professor James Woodrow, who aroused in Lanier an interest in German lyric poetry and idealistic philosophy, and a continuing interest in trying to reconcile evolutionary thought with Presbyterian theology.

His tentative writings and, possibly more important, his plans to study in Germany were abruptly terminated by the outbreak of war. He returned briefly in 1863 to writing poems (inspired mainly by his love for Virginia Hankins) and to translating lyrics by Heine and Herder, but in the main, during this lull in his military activities, such literary energy as he could summon forth was devoted to his projected novel, *Tiger-Lilies* (1867). Somewhat oddly, it is in this prose rather than in his verse that Lanier has his best-sustained image, that of the blood-red flower of war (Book II, Chapter 1).

Lanier's work, in this novel as well as in his poetry, is a curious mixture of nineteenth-century thought and antique vocabulary. He was at once a high-hearted if belated Romantic and a devout Medievalist. Shakspere and Chaucer seemed beyond question the greatest of English poets, if not indeed the greatest of poets. He advised Paul

Hamilton Hayne that to develop properly as a poet he must "drink much of Chaucer and little of Morris"; and he made such extensive use of Shaksperean imagery that Aubrey Starke (283) credited him with so developing "the use of the Shaksperean imagery in description of nature as to develop what is almost a distinct genre."

In spite of his fascination with medievalism and his late, symbolic use of Bishop Aldheim as "the Father of English Poetry," he belonged essentially to his own time. To Lanier, poetry had improved primarily by becoming more ethereal, more spirit-like. This seemed good; it led him at times, rather disconcertingly, to place Tennyson above Milton: "To discover the process of spiritualization which poetry has undergone, one has only to compare Tennyson with Milton. . . . Milton's is the strength of the sea in its rage; Tennyson's is the potential force of the sea in its repose" (V, 326–27).

Closely allied with his theory that as time flows on "sensuous things constantly etherealize" was his concept of metaphor. It was true that a metaphor was "always a union of two objects." but he also believed that metaphors "come of love rather than of thought." One object was normally abstract, the other concrete, so that the "nature-metaphor is a beautiful eternal bridal of spirit and matter . . . . this harmonious union of soul and body, of spirit and nature, of essence and form, is promoted by the nature-metaphor" (V, 306–21).

It was not poetic theories but Reconstruction that aroused him to an authentic if brief lyricism. The best of these poems, "The Raven Days," states with precise power the hopelessness of men who felt themselves betrayed into "hatred and bitterness as even the four terrible years of war had entirely failed to bring about." The poem ends with a question: will these dark raven days of sorrow be replaced by a warm light that will "gleam across the

mournful plain?" More complex in structure and therefore indirect in statement is "Night and Day." Othello
personifies night, but he also stands for the Civil War and
for Reconstruction; the dark Moor (night) has murdered
Desdemona (day), and at the same time he (as the dual
strife of warfare and of reconstruction) has slain peace—
and Lanier could see little hope that the "Star-memories
of happier times" would soon return to his harassed
region. The Shaksperean imagery is not merely a literary
device; it is integral to the meaning of the poem (I, 15,
160).

Although weaker in quality, two other poems about
Reconstruction deserve to be mentioned. "Tyranny" is a
bitter attack on the economic decay (a stagnation that
Lanier likens to death) that pervaded the South. There is
no use for the spring-germs except to stay and "feed the
worms"; the heat of summer would avail only to bake a
barren land. The eight-line "Ship of Earth" might, except
for the 1868 date and the companion poems, be read as
generalized philosophy of a somewhat obvious nature,
with the earth's need for a pilot since "the helm is left
awry,/ And the best sailors in the ship lie there among
the dead." The final line is true at any time, in any place,
but Lanier had specifically in mind the leaderless South
and the need for strong guidance and direction to lead a
harried, down-trodden region away from destruction and
set it back on a course that would lead to life and to hope.
The more directly autobiographical poem "Barnacles,"
with its appeal to an encumbering Past to free him from
its dead shells, belongs to the same period and may have
the same unhappy, immediate period in mind, but the
poetic statement is so generalized that it hardly seems relevant except as personal protest (I, 11–15).

Intermittently in the period from 1868 through 1874,
Lanier devoted much of his poetic time and thought to a

projected "novel in verse, with several lyric poems introduced by the action. The plot is founded on what was
called 'the Jacquerie,' a very remarkable popular insurrection wh. happened in France about the year 1359, in the
height of Chivalry" (VII, 307). This never-completed
work was meant to be an attack on Trade and a plea for
the restoration of Chivalry; from the surviving fragments,
it seems unlikely that it would ever have become his
magnum opus. But one lyric deserves to rank with his
best: "The hound was cuffed, the hound was kicked."
The revolting peasants are symbolized by the hound
which kills its master, and for once Lanier works entirely
through his image. It is necessary to know the first twenty-
four lines of the narrative for the lyric to become clear,
but with this background the clean-cut imagery reinforces
the tragic situation (See IX, 121–22).

An intensely personal poem, "Life and Song" (first entitled, significantly, "Work and Song"), describes the
ideal union of life and art, a fusion that would result in
wholeness. Indirectly, the poem expresses a bitter realization that he himself, in those poverty-stricken, troubled
days, could not attain this harmony. The affirmation of
faith in poetry and music is curiously balanced, yet en-
riched, by the note of personal renunciation (I, 16).

These seem the best of his early lyrics. Aubrey Starke
(147) preferred "Nirvâna," reading into Lanier's quest
for spiritual contentment an epithalamium for Mary Day
Lanier: "marriage to her more than anything else in his
life brought to Lanier the enraptured ecstasy and the
sense of escape from the terrors of contemporary events
which he so subtly conveys to us in this poem." This is an
attractive reading, although it hardly jibes with Lanier's
explanation to Virginia Hankins that "Of course it is a
rapt Hindu who speaks" (I, 335). But the erroneous conception of Nirvâna as the "Highest Paradise of Buddha,

attainable only by long contemplation, and by perfect
superiority to all passions of men and all vicissitudes of
Time" (instead of a state of non-existence) has proved a
stumbling-block to many readers. Possibly the didactic,
declamatory tone harms it even more as a poem (I,
19–21).

The most popular of his early poems was "Thar's More
in the Man Than Thar Is in the Land," published in the
Macon *Telegraph and Messenger,* February 7, 1871, and
widely though often anonymously reprinted. It is written
in the dialect of a Georgia Cracker, and it has humorous
overtones and poetic trickeries (Lanier rhymes *hum—*
with *cum* and *sum,* and begins the next line with *Ble*).
But the poem is fundamentally serious. It was in fact the
best of several dialect poems using the thesis that a plantation economy based on cotton had harmed if not ruined
the South financially, and that the region must change the
pattern to one of small farms and diversified agriculture.
Unlike Henry Grady, he did not want an industrialized
South; in direct contrast with the early war poems of
Henry Timrod, Lanier had no faith in "the snow of
Southern summers." Cotton was a money crop, dependent
on trade—and he had come to hate everything connected
with his concept of trade. In the narrative poem the
Cracker Jones, who "lived pretty much by gittin' of
loans," goes bankrupt first in Georgia and five years later
in Texas, but Brown revitalized the rundown, eroded
Georgia farm and made it pay by hard work and by plant-
ing wheat and corn. Lanier extends the diversification in
"The Homestead" (which is not in dialect) to include
fruit, cattle, chickens, hogs, and pastures, so that the farm
becomes almost self-sustaining. But the major symbol of
this diversification, in his mind, was corn, as cotton was
the major symbol of the one-crop, money economy (I,
22–23, 25–28).

The poems in Negro dialect were primarily humorous. "The Power of Prayer," written in collaboration with his brother Clifford, is the story of an old blind Negro and presumably his young granddaughter who mistake for the devil the noise of the first steamboat coming up the Alabama River. When the boat rounds the bend and with diminishing noise proceeds upstream, the old Negro is convinced that through prayer he has foiled "the debble." There are primitive though authentic religious overtones, but these are subordinated to the humor. The poem was published in *Scribner's* (which also published the collaborative "Uncle Jim's Baptist Revival Hymn") and widely reprinted, but Lanier was doubtful of the validity of dialect poetry. He wrote to Charlotte Cushman: "Tell me, *ought* one to be a little ashamed of writing a dialect poem?" Although Pattee called Lanier "a pioneer in a rich field," he seems to have abandoned dialect with a feeling of relief (I, 215–17); however, in 1879 he corrected the Negro dialect in a poem by another author for *Scribner's Monthly* (X, 156).

Perhaps these poems should have freed Lanier from his fondness for archaic and sentimentalized phraseology. They did not. Instead, his growing absorption in music led to a discontent with conventional rhythm and metre. When in March 1874, he sent his wife "My Two Springs," he apparently was content with such phrases as "And home-loves and high glory-loves/ And science-loves and story-loves," and in the last stanza he reduces the otherwise excellent imagery by explicitly describing the springs as the eyes of Mary Day Lanier. His discontent took another form: "since I have written it to print, I cannot make it such as I desire in artistic design; for the forms of to-day require a certain trim smugness and clean-shaven propriety in the face and dress of a poem and I must win a hearing by conforming in some degree to these tyran-

nies, with a view to overturning them in the future." Yet
a certain trimness was almost inevitable as long as he lived
up to his profound belief that "all lyric poetry must be"
sweet, brief, passionate "outgleamings of melody . . . each
poem expressing but a single idea, and expressing that in
the shortest manner possible, and in the simplest, noblest,
most beautiful, and most musical words" (I, 32–34; IX,
35, 39–40). These were at best but "short swallow flights
of song."

One solution was to write longer and more ambitious
poems in which he could develop related forms in varied
metrical patterns, and impose a less formal unity through
an architectonic structure. His first rather mild attempt
was in the Pindaric or Cowleyan ode, "Corn." The lines
are of irregular lengths, but the prevailing pattern is
iambic and most lines fall into normal two-feet to five-feet
accentual lengths; ordinarily, three consecutive lines have
perfect end-rhymes, usually monosyllabic, but these triple
rhymes are carefully interspersed with contrasting rhyming couplets. "Corn" represents an advance in his command of metrical effects in a freer, more easily flowing
verse, but primarily in a longer, sustained, unified effort.

The structure of the poem has less unity. Lanier's
friend Logan E. Bleckley complained that Lanier presented four landscapes, the first two in an Italian vein and
painted "with the utmost delicacy and finish. . . . When
you paint in Dutch or Flemish you are clear and strong,
but sometimes hard." William Dean Howells in rejecting
it for the *Atlantic* thought it was basically two poems but
that "neither was striking enough to stand alone." (Both
quoted in Starke, 189.) There is some justice in these statements. The poem begins with the poet wandering
through a forest and describing the beauties of the trees
and the undergrowth, although there is also a hint of his
developing pantheism and fondness for personification in

the lines, "I pray with mosses, ferns and flowers shy/ That hide like gentle nuns from human eye/ To lift adoring perfumes to the sky." The poet wanders to a zigzag fence separating the forest and a cornfield; he takes an aesthetic delight in its beauty: "without theft, I reap another's field." One tall stalk of corn is completely out of line; again personifying, Lanier reads into this "corn-captain" a kinship with the poet. The stalk is rooted in earth, yet reaches toward heaven; similarly, the poet should be rooted in the local and the particular, but should give to other men universal values by marrying the new and the old, by uniting earth and heaven, and by reconciling the hot and the cold, the dark and the bright in human lives.

Then Lanier shifts to his harshest direct attack on cotton as symbolic of agricultural trade. Cotton has been responsible for soil erosion; worse, it has been responsible for unstable, discontented lives. The cotton farmer is a "foolish Jason on a treacherous sea,/ Seeking the Fleece and finding misery." Instead of secure, self-contained farming, he "staked his life on games of Buy-and-Sell,/ and turned each field into a gambler's hell," until he became a "gamester's catspaw and a banker's slave."

The final section is addressed to the eroded old hill. Once again, Lanier's indifference to the logic of his images is only too readily discernible, along with his fondness for literary personifications. The hill becomes a "gashed and hairy Lear," but his daughter Cordelia becomes the rejuvenating, pitying Spring. Perhaps Lanier considered this a union of matter and spirit, but it seems at best a strange yoking-together of a father and daughter. Spring and corn will re-vitalize the wornout land. Perhaps Lanier thought of corn as symbolic of diversified farming; perhaps he over-simplified because of the beauty of the cornfield; but within the framework of the concluding section there is no hint that corn by itself will not enrich eroded land (I, 34–39).

In spite of defects in structure and in logical development, "Corn" remains the first of Lanier's major poems. The forest and the cornfield are vividly described, the attack on cotton sharp and readable. The nature-personifications are effective, although they only indicate a way that Lanier was to explore more fully in later works. When "Corn" was published in *Lippincott's Magazine* (February 1875) and enthusiastically praised by the discerning Gilbert Peacock, it justifiably earned for Lanier a reputation as a poet of national importance.

In 1875 he wrote and published in *Lippincott's* one of his most ambitious poems, "The Symphony." The title may be an unfortunate one. It has led various commentators to object that the poem does not have the form of a symphony, thus implying that Lanier failed to achieve his objective. This is a misreading. The poem is meant to be a part (not all) of a performance or rehearsal; rarely, and then only for a few consecutive lines, does the entire orchestra play together. It is mainly a series of solo performances, by six different instruments.

As he noted, the poem treated "various deep social questions of the time," and it had in the writing taken possession of him "like a real James River Ague" (IX, 182). But the work was no hasty improvisation; on the contrary, it was carefully wrought and its effect premeditated. For the first time Lanier attempted freely to make words do the work of music. Drawing on a Shaksperean sonnet for an allusion, he noted that "In my 'Symphony', Love's fine wit—the love of one's fellow-men—attempts (not to hear with eyes, but precisely the reverse) to see with ears" (IX, 319). For this purpose he used many and varying devices of versification. In the opening section, the prevailing four-beat iambic line is broken with short lines, one with a truncated foot: "Tráde is tráde." There is a skillful use of two and three line end-rhymes, but there is also an occasional use of internal rhymes. More noticeable, and reflecting his recent study of Anglo-Saxon poetry, is the heavy monotone of alliteration. Both of these can be illustrated by one couplet:

Of what avail the rigorous tale
Of bill for coin and box for bale? (I, 46)

Later in the poem, when the knight promises to do battle for the lady, Lanier uses the form of a traditional medieval song, with its insistent refrain of "Fair Lady." The concluding sections contrast with this fixed pattern by their deliberate irregularity. Lanier declared that he had "Dared *almost* to write quite at my ease in the matters of rhythm, rhyme, and substance, in this poem," and he had largely succeeded (IX, 203).

In spite of the intricate metrical effects, Lanier seems to have been even more interested in the message than in the form. Yet the subject is not simple, but complicated with a series of related and intertwined ideas. The primary one, an attack on trade and materialism, had obsessed him since he had started struggling with "The Jacquerie," seven or eight years earlier. There is also a statement of his new-found belief that God reveals himself through nature, and this revelation must be translated for most men not through the Church but through art: "Where Nature spreads her wild blue sky/ For Art to make into melody!" More clearly stated is the demand for a restoration of chivalry in the world. But the overriding message, not in fact economic, is for a broader and deeper human love, supported by a more intense, deeply-felt (if unorthodox) religion.

The poem develops through personifications. The violins and, quickly, the other strings, personify art; the flute, nature; the clarionet, the lady; the horn, the knight; the hautboy, the child (almost equated with Christ); the concluding bassoons, wise old age. The violins begin the attack on trade, but immediately suggest Lanier's metaphysical solution: "O Trade! O Trade! would thou wert dead!/ The time needs heart—'tis tired of head." Love has been overcome by greed that has degenerated into swinehood at the expense of humanity. Men have for too long disregarded Christ's words, *"Man shall not live by bread alone."* For trade has no mercy. The mistreated and the underpaid can easily be replaced, since the poor are prolific. Trade has become only "war grown miserly," but the solution is not in economics but in love: "Vainly might Plato's brain revolve it;/ Plainly the heart of a child could solve it."

After a brief interlude by the orchestra, the flute is introduced with what seems to me Lanier's finest, best-sustained poetic image:

> But presently
> A velvet flute-note fell down pleasantly
> Upon the bosom of that harmony,
> And sailed and sailed incessantly,
> As if a petal from a wild-rose blown
> Had fluttered down upon that pool of tone
> And boatwise dropped o' the convex side
> And floated down the glassy tide
> And clarified and glorified
> The solemn spaces where the shadows bide. (I, 48–49)

The flute states precisely its own function in the poem: "I hold/ Full powers from Nature manifold" to speak for the great and the small, for the "no-tongued tree," the lichens, mosses, ferns. This power extends also to animate birds, animals, and insects, and even to the sound of the wind through the trees. The flute holds that man had once been in harmony with nature, but this equilibrium had been upset in ancient times by false mythologies and pagan religions—"cold creatures of man's colder brain." This separation from true nature continued until Christ proclaimed "Love thy neighbor . . . *All men are neigh-bors.*" Then man briefly could understand nature and be at peace with mountains, rivers, trees, and with each other. But trade had again distorted this harmonious relationship, and it could be restored only through love.

The clarionet blames trade for debasing the purity of womanhood and introducing prostitution into the world, and the horn promises through the re-vivification of chivalry to restore her to her rightful place in the world. As trade has warped our relations with religion and with nature, so it has warped our relations with each other. The hautboy, speaking for the child, quotes Christ after introductory words that suggest Lanier had given up his earlier faith in Christ's divinity: "Once said a Man—and wise was He—/*Never shalt thou the heavens see,/ Save as a little child thou be.*"

The bassoons conclude the poem. Life itself is like a fugue, from birth to death (east to west), but the musical score is not freshly made; it is a continuum with "harsh half-phrasings,/ Blotted ere writ," a "weltering palimpsest" dimly recording all that has gone before. Only through love can the discords be resolved. As early as *Tiger-Lilies* Lanier had written that "Music means harmony, harmony means love, and love means—God" (V, 31). At the end of "The Symphony" he returned to that theme. Drawing on his belief that man and nature steadily etherealize, he closed on a note of optimism, with an allusion to the Biblical flood: "O'er the modern waste a dove hath whirred:/ Music is love in search of a word" (I, 45–56).

"The Symphony" won him new friends in Philadelphia, most notably Bayard Taylor. Mainly through the intercession of Taylor, Lanier was commissioned to write the verses for a cantata to be sung at the Centennial Exposition in Philadelphia, the music to be composed by

Dudley Buck. Although Taylor cautioned him to "make the lines simple and strong" and to make the poem representative rather than individualistic, Lanier disregarded his advice. As a musician himself, he felt that he had "to compose for the musician as well as the country" not in clearly-stated lines but in *"broad bands of color"* (IX, 297). The poem, entitled "The Centennial Meditation of Columbia," celebrates America as a haven for those oppressed by religious or economic tyranny; names like Mayflower, Plymouth, Jamestown, Puritan, and Huguenot become in themselves symbols. There are eight contrasting stanzas in words mainly of Saxon derivation, beginning with the early difficulties of colonization and concluding with "the Triumph of the Republic over the opposing powers of nature and of man." Although he complained that limitations of space allowed him to devote only one line each to the philosophies of Art, Science, Power, Government, Faith, and Social Life, he thought that he had made it "absolutely free from all melodramatic artifice, and wholly simple and artless" (II, 271; IX, 300, 311, 353).

When the poem was published without the music, it was immediately attacked as obscure and vague, with archaic words and stilted hyphenations, as in the lines "Toil when wild brother-wars new-dark the Light,/ Toil, and forgive, and kiss o'er, and replight." Lanier defended the work vigorously: it was meant to be sung rather than to be read. He felt vindicated when, sung by a chorus of eight hundred voices to the accompaniment of one hundred fifty instruments, the cantata was a dramatic success (I, 60–62).

Lippincott's commissioned Lanier to write a centennial ode for its July 1876 issue. "Psalm of the West" is his longest complete poem, but it is also his most disjointed one. There is some excuse. It was written hurriedly, at a

time when he was ill. Yet the good qualities in the poem
are typical of Lanier, and so are the defects. As Aubrey
Starke has noted (248), Lanier had attempted "to compose a poem which should carry or create its own musical
accompaniment." The beginning is conventional enough.
America is the "Tall Adam of lands, new-made of the dust
of the West," from whose side Eve (Freedom) is carved.
It is freedom that gives power to Friendship, Marriage,
Law, and other human attributes:

> And Science be known as the sense making love to the
>   All.
> And Art be known as the soul making love to the All,
> And Love be known as the marriage of man with the All.
>   (I, 63)

God will help this All-lover, the prophet and poet, the
"lark of the dawn," by revealing to him the past and the
future. Disregarding the Indians, Lanier celebrates in a
ballad-like interlude the coming of the Norsemen, and in
eight Miltonic sonnets the first voyage of Columbus (cast
in the form of a dramatic monologue and narrated by
Columbus himself). After the discovery, the colonization
is symbolized in the poem by the Mayflower, and the war
for independence is worked mainly around the battle at
Lexington. Lanier notes in passing that Jefferson had told
"the rights of man to men" and that "Deep-rooted Washington" had won final success at Yorktown. In his haste,
and perhaps because he did not wish to mar the national-
istic tone of the ode by discussing the issues and differences involved, Lanier incorporated a much earlier poem
as an allegory of the Civil War. If "The Tournament:
Joust First" was written, as Anderson thinks, in 1865 as a
peace-offering to the estranged Mary Day, this conflict between heart and brain may have been appropriate; as an
allegory of the Civil War, it is both absurd and insipid.
Wisely Lanier hastens on to the prophecy, as revealed by

the artist's God: in this reunited land Freedom will drive out the beasts of War, Oppression, Murder, Lust, False Art, and False Faith (I, 62–82).

"Psalm of the West" is not a philosophical poem, but a series of pen-pictures that Lanier thought to be representative and tried to make symbolic. He succeeded best with the sonnet-sequence. But he failed to impose an artistic unity on his diverse, unconnected forms and incidents, and his enthusiastic paean of over-optimistic prophecy is difficult to read seriously. But the poem solidified his reputation. This was further consolidated when later that year Lippincott issued in book form ten of his poems that had appeared in *Lippincott's Magazine,* including "Corn," "The Symphony," and "Psalm."

Temporarily abandoning his theories of musical versification, Lanier wrote in blank verse a long poem, "Clover." It embodied his artistic creed, and he later planned to use it as the title poem of a projected volume. It grew, he wrote, "out of a mood of solemn protest against the doctrine of 'Art for Art's Sake,' which has led so many of our young artists into the most unprofitable and even blasphemous activities" (IX, 398, *n.*135). But it grew also out of his wrathful memories of the attacks on the Centennial Cantata, and he twice gives a list of fellow-artists who had likewise been mistreated: Dante, Keats, Chopin, Raphael, Lucretius, Omar, Angelo, Beethoven, Chaucer, Schubert, Shakspere, Bach, and Buddha. As the materialistic ox destroys the clover, so the Course-of-things destroys the artist. Only faith that we are all part of God's plan will save us, with the realization that "The artist's market is the heart of man." It is a troubled, uneven poem, yet it is easy to see why Lanier overvalued it (I, 84–87).

That same year he wrote the most beautiful of the many lyrics to his wife, "Evening Song" (set to music by

Dudley Buck under the title "Sunset"). Lanier's love poems rarely measure up to his best lyrics, but this dainty, tranquil poem is an exception. However, Lanier's poetic well was, temporarily, almost dry. Of the poems written in 1877, only two can be considered even reasonably successful. In "The Stirrup-Cup," death becomes a rare cordial handed to the horseman just before he sets out on a long journey. The appropriate metaphor, the literary allusions, and the gallant courage of a sick man willing to drink the "rich stirrup-cup . . . right smilingly" gives the lyric an enduring if somewhat personalized appeal. The second poem is more important and has become his best-known poem. The "Song of the Chattahoochee" is Lanier's extreme use of personification, for throughout, the river is the narrator; the onomatopoeia and the heavy use of the refrain testify to Poe's continuing influence; and the interlocking vowel and consonant sounds, the alliteration, and the internal rhymes indicate Lanier's desire for musicality at the expense of idea. The poem does have a lulling motion that has a narcotic effect on many readers. But the objection that the personification is a pathetic fallacy overlooks the fact that only this justifies Lanier in giving the Chattahoochee a moral duty to water the fields and turn the mills, before it at last becomes a part of the ocean (I, 88, 90, 103–104).

Lanier had becoming increasingly fascinated with the running or logaoedic dactyllic measure, which in his definition allowed a free admixture of iambics and spondees. "The Revenge of Hamish" he considered frankly "an experiment" in this metre (X, 72). The subject was derived practically without change from Chapter II of William Black's novel, *MacLeod of Dare;* the four-line stanza form and the rhyme scheme of this narrative poem suggest the medieval ballad, but the long, looping lines, the free metre, and varying rhythms are Lanier's own additions. It

is a quick-moving, interesting story in verse of a brutal
punishment and an even more brutal revenge, but it is
quite uncharacteristic of Lanier's other poetry.

Time spent in or near Brunswick, Georgia, alongside
the Marshes of Glynn, revived his poetic imagination. He
planned a series of Hymns of the Marshes, to be either a
separate book or combined with related (and mainly un-
written) Hymns of the Fields and Hymns of the Mountains. Easily the best of these—in fact, his best long poem
—is "The Marshes of Glynn." The form is an even freer
use than in "The Revenge" of the logaoedic dactyl—so
free that at times the pattern disappears, ranging from the
prevailing pentameter rhyming couplets to a one-syllabled
line. It is also most intricate musically, for as Norman
Foerster has perceptively pointed out (*Nature in American Literature*, 235), it is "not one melody artfully
varied, but a bewildering succession of winding and dart-
ing melodies." The effect is orchestral rather than har-
monic. Lanier begins with the feeling of ecstasy aroused
by the live-oaks and the marshes; he almost equates the
oak with the Holy Ghost, as he was to equate the marsh
with what he could accept of the primal beginning in the
theory of evolution. It is evening, but he has secured a
spiritual release from the finite world:

> Ay, now, when my soul all day hath drunken the soul of
>   the oak,
> And my heart is at ease from men, and the wearisome
>   sound of the stroke
>   Of the scythe of time and the trowel of trade is low,
>   And belief overmasters doubt, and I know that I
>   know,
>   And my spirit is grown to a lordly great compass
>   within,
>   That the length and the breadth and the sweep of the
>   marshes of Glynn
>   Will work me no fear like the fear they have wrought
>   me of yore. . . . (I, 119)

In the enormously long first sentence, nature personified
in the live oak is good, the essence of spiritual comfort;
trade and finite time are evil. To the east is the ocean, to
Lanier a symbol of infinity; in the east, also, was the beginning of the world. The recognition of this gives him
faith, and a new-found freedom from doubt. The marsh
now seems to him like the catholic man who has won
"God out of knowledge and good out of infinite pain/
And sight out of blindness and purity out of a stain."

In another of his curiously-mixed metaphors in which
he tried to weld together the concrete and the abstract,
Lanier continues: "As the marsh-hen secretly builds on
the watery sod,/ Behold I will build me a nest on the
greatness of God." This simile, widely and disconcertingly
praised by many high school teachers, is the low point
in the poem. Fortunately, Lanier soon recovers from this
illogical sentimentality. The incoming tide serves a triple
purpose: literally, the ocean floods the marsh, but figura-
tively the infinite floods the finite, and thus floods the soul
of man so that he attains union with God. Yet the poem
ends on a note of doubt. The high tide brings with it
night and sleep, with its suggestion of death:

> But who will reveal to our waking ken
> The forms that swim and the shapes that creep
>   Under the waters of sleep?
> And I would I could know what swimmeth below when
>   the tide comes in
> On the length and the breadth of the marvellous
>   marshes of Glynn. (I, 122)

This probing into the subconscious is uncharacteristic; so
too is the element of doubt. "The Marshes of Glynn" is
the final complete poem in the sequence. He intended to
open the Hymns with "Sunrise" (written later), but it
seems unlikely that he intended to close on this note.
There is no way to know, but I am convinced that one of

his most complete Poem Outlines at least indicates the direction the concluding poem would have taken:

> The courses of the wind, and the shifts thereof, as also what way the clouds go; and that which is happening a long way off; and the full face of the sun; and the bow of the Milky Way from end to end; as also the small, the life of the fiddler-crab, and the household of the marsh-hen; yes, and more, the translation of black ooze into green blade of marsh-grass, which is as if filth bred heaven:
> This a man seeth upon the marsh (I, 276).

That the marsh had become a symbol in his mind of the condition from which man had developed (not evolved) is indicated by a letter about another poem in the sequence:

> For whatever can be proved to have been evolved, evolution seems to me a noble and beautiful and true theory. But a careful search has not shown me a single instance . . . of an actual case of species differentiation (X, 205).

A man was free to make his own choices; he was not a biological pawn in a pre-determined game. In fact, Lanier was developing a theory of opposing forces in nature. All the motions in nature resulted from this opposition or antagonism of forces, and from this opposition came rhythm. This seemed to justify his belief in a freer form for poetry and music: following Herbert Spencer's *First Principles,* he believed evolution to be "a process from the uniform and indefinite to the multiform and definite." It did not justify formlessness: he quoted with approval and worked changes on the aphorism of the French poet Hervé that "He who will not answer to the rudder, must answer to the rocks." Aubrey Starke (372) has neatly phrased Lanier's principle of opposition as "Form against Chaos, of Good against Evil, of Love against Selfishness, of

Design against Accident, of Belief against Scepticism."
This "fundamental principle of creation" he embodied in
the poem "Opposition." It is through the conquest of
these adverse forces that man's will, his moral sense, and
his art develop:

> Of fret, of dark, of thorn, of chill,
>   Complain no more; for these, O Heart,
> Direct the random of the will
>   As rhymes direct the rage of art. (I, 130-31)

It is an abstractly philosophical idea which Lanier developed in *The Science of English Verse,* but which he
nowhere stated more appealingly than in this lyric.

Although he shied away from theology, Lanier's mind
was engrossed by religious problems. "Remonstrance" is a
bitterly personal objection to "Prim Creed," and his attempt to find, vainly, spiritual food in the church service.
There were bitter divisions: to the Protestants, *"Religion
hath blue eyes and yellow hair:*/ She's Saxon, all." To the
Catholic, *"Religion hath black eyes and raven hair:*/
Nought else is true." This racial over-simplification of the
two dominant religions in the western world, the poet
declares, leaves only love as solace, but even that fails
him:

> I homeward turn, my fires of pain to slake
>   In deep endearments of a worshipped wife.
>   "I love thee well, dear Love," quoth she, "and yet
> Would that thy creed with mine completely met,
>   As one, not two." (I, 123)

Human love, and faith in the Lord as revealed in the stars
and the earth, are his only consolation. The poet asks
only, but with little hope, that the organized Church and
the formalized, inhuman creeds let him alone, to work out
his own salvation through divine and through human love
(I, 122–24).

Out of this preoccupation came, also, the long, humorless poem "The Crystal," with its odd spectacle of a minor poet forgiving, among many others, Dante, Shakspere, and Milton. Although Juliet's "prurient pun" about death in the sexual rather than the literal sense especially offended his tight-lipped morality, he objected also (considering his own poetry, ironically) to Shakspere's "fustian" rhetoric, and even to his acceptance of the dramatic convention that allowed women to "mask as men." But it was the "labor-lewd discourse" that particularly troubled him. Some other comments are useful in revealing Lanier's critical prejudices. Homer had been guilty of "sandy wastes of prose and catalogue"; Socrates of "iron stringencies" when milder words would have wrought a finer effect; Buddha had for "needy man . . . Nothing"; "worn Dante" revealed his own "implacable hates . . . in thy horrid hells"; Milton with his "comic-dreadful wars" had filled "all heaven with folly." He goes on to call the roll of slightly lesser writers: Aeschylus had no concept of love; Lucretius only a poor logic; Marcus Aurelius, Thomas à Kempis, Epictetus, Swedenborg, Langley, and Caedmon for all their excellences were somehow too remote from ordinary men. In his own time, Emerson, in "finding Wisdom, lost/ Thy Self, sometimes"; Keats was too tense; even Tennyson, the "largest voice/ Since Milton" had "some register of wit/ Wanting" (as in his consideration of Poe, Lanier means that Tennyson lacked the seer-like quality which he felt the greatest writers must have).

It is an impressive listing of great writers, but it reveals how little Lanier comprehended of their true greatness. True, this recognition of their fallibility leads up to the infallibility and perfection of Christ the man. It is Lanier's clearest statement that he had come to regard Christ as symbol of divinity, but not divine (I, 136–39). The conflict in his mind between religion and science resulted in the kindred poem, "The Cloud," with its strong affirmation that while a cloud might be evolved, an artist could not be: he was a free and responsible being, yet answerable to himself, to mankind, and to God for the work he produced. The earlier title, "Individuality," better describes the idea that Lanier stressed; apparently he changed the title when he decided to incorporate the poem into the "Hymns of the Marshes" (I, 136–41).

He was to write two more magnificent lyrics, and a long, fevered poem. "Marsh Song—at Sunset" depends on a reasonable familiarity with *The Tempest*, but once again, as in "Night and Day," the Shaksperean imagery serves as a springboard to lead to his essential idea. It is an Ariel-cloud and a Caliban-sea, but it is not the brother or the man Antonio who has injured Prospero; rather it is Antonio as man who has committed the injustice and it is man in general (not a specific person) who must be pardoned. The narrator seems in fact to be a personification of Nature, whom man has injured by getting out of harmony with it; if this interpretation is correct, it is nature in the last line who says, "Brother, I pardon thee." In Lanier's interpretation, it is not so much malignancy as lack of understanding of the essential goodness and the divinely revelatory power of nature that has made man an almost unwitting culprit. Lanier was adapting *The Tempest* to his own purposes.

He followed this with the quickly-written, intricately musical "Ballad of Trees and the Master." Ironically, with apparently no attention to what it says, the poem is included in a Methodist Hymnal, and frequently sung. It is Lanier's finest yet most extreme statement that God reveals himself to man not through the church but through nature. On the eve of his crucifixion, a disturbed and "forspent" Christ goes into the woods, and it is the olive trees that console Christ and give him strength to endure his ordeal. Like the live-oak in "The Marshes of Glynn,"

the trees become synonymous with the Holy Spirit. It is
Lanier's most beautiful lyric, one that we could not easily
spare from our scant number of nearly perfect poems (I,
142, 144).

He had no chance fully to revise his last poem, "Sunrise." He intended it to be the first poem in "Hymns of the
Marshes," and it is optimistic about the place man has attained in the world. Before he awakes, the poet is con-
scious of three major symbols: the live-oak, the marsh,
and the main. The live-oak brings God to man; the marsh
is that from which man has evolved; and the ocean is
immortality. In this sense the marsh is indeed a "Reverend Marsh," a menstruum that dissolves and re-creates all
matter. But a fourth major symbol, even more important
than the earlier three, is added. The sun is equated with
Christ; it is the life-giving force that makes the "sacra-
mental marsh one pious plain." Before the rising of the
sun there is the quiet stillness of dawn, the "ante-reign of
Mary Morning." Then the sun, which gives to man a
strength that even the live-oak can not give: "I am strong
with the strength of my lord the Sun." And the sun even
more than the main gives us conviction of immortality:
after death, "Yonder besides thee/ My soul shall float,
friend Sun,/ The day being done."

This is perhaps his strongest poetic statement, though
by no means his only one, of his belief in a personal immortality. He could not accept the "marvellous delusion"
of Emerson that "personality is to die away into the first
cause" (IV, 165–66). Instead, the individual was poten-
tially divine, and would retain his individuality after
death. Charles R. Anderson has rightly stated that

> "Sunrise" is a summing up of Lanier as both man and
> poet. Here his courage in facing death has become trium-
> phant acceptance, the social gospel of "The Symphony"
> has been transmuted into a chant for a better world sung
> with the conviction of poetic vision rather than the

querulousness of the reformer, the adoration of nature has been exalted into unqualified worship of the sun as the divine source of life—but also as the symbol of immorality (I, lxv; see also I, 262–68, 271).

It was the last, fitting testament of an unorthodox but deeply religious man.

✓ Any re-evaluation of Lanier as poet might well start with his admitted weaknesses. These can be listed briefly: (1) a strong tendency toward moralizing and didacticism, sometimes combined with an excessive, lushly-phrased sentimentalism, especially when these elements are not part of the texture of the poem but are added on rather obtrusively; (2) a frequent use of over-fervid rhetoric as a substitute for imagination, as in the Sun-Bee passage in "Sunrise"; (3) a strained imagery that grew out of Lanier's desire to yoke together in one metaphor the concrete and the abstract; (4) the use of archaic words and constructions that, although characteristic of Lanier's thought, give a quaint, artificial character to many poems.

Such handicaps are severe. Yet they do not ruin, even if they do vitiate, his positive accomplishment. The best of the long poems have sufficient intellectual philosophical content and enough musical form to lift them above their inherent defects. At their best, they have also a strong sense of locale, derived from exact and sympathetic observation. "Corn" is a spirited economic protest against the agricultural money-crop cotton, and a strong plea for diversified agriculture; the description of the woods and of the cornfield is what Lanier had seen closely with his own eyes before he turned the raw matter into poetry. On a wider base, "The Symphony" is both an economic and a social protest; one may not agree with his concept that trade (materialism) inevitably debases or that nature etherealizes, but certainly there is no lack of valid subject-matter. Yet it is as a religious poet that Lanier in his

longer poems is at his best. All four are loosely constructed, and marred by rhetorical flourishes and illogical
images. But the disordered though powerful "Sunrise"
and the magnificent "Marshes of Glynn" express Lanier's
mature religious belief: God is immanent, and he reveals
himself to us through nature, in the ferns, the streams, the
marsh, the trees, and the sun. When he complained that
Poe did not know enough "to be a great poet," Lanier
was not thinking of practical or scholarly knowledge, but
of that intuitive comprehension by which a poet converts
learning into wisdom (II, 6; VII, 94–96). This was what
he attempted to do, and in "The Marshes of Glynn" he
largely succeeded.

These faults cannot be found in a handful of his best
lyrics. The early poems ("Night and Day," "Raven Days,"
"Life and Song," and one or two dialect poems) are sim-
pler but not necessarily poorer than the later lyrics. He
had not yet begun, in theory and in practice, to loosen the
structure of English versification. As he developed, he
found it hampering and nearly impossible to stay within a
rigid framework: except for the Columbus sonnets in
"Psalm of the West" and possibly "The Harlequin of
Dreams," he wrote no sonnets that are comparable to
those of Longfellow, Boker, and Hayne. He preferred to
depend on musical cadence and a trained ear rather than
on accent or rhythm; at times he may have carried this
over into artifice, as in "Song of the Chattahoochee," but
at his best ("Evening Song," "Marsh Song," and above
all, "Ballad of Trees") he wrote some of the finest lyrics
in American poetry.

It is a thin sheaf of authentic poetry that we can salvage
from the occasional and the sentimental, but it remains an
authentic one. Lanier never attained his goal of writing
major poetry, but he wrote a small number of poems that
have never received the recognition they deserved. He is
one of our most vital and most interesting minor poets.

III   *The Critic*

At the beginning, it needs to be kept in mind that only a small part of Lanier's criticism was written for publication. Even *The Science of English Verse,* which appeared during his lifetime, soon came to seem inadequate and he planned to revise it. A few critical articles were published in magazines, but he wrote more on travel and music than he did on literature. The bulk of his writing was merely drafts for his lecture courses, and one title, *The English Novel,* was imposed upon the book by his publishers in lieu of Lanier's more cumbersome but more descriptive title: *From Aeschylus to George Eliot: Twelve Studies in the Modern English Novel as a Development of the Greek Drama.* Lanier's reputation as a literary critic would probably be higher and certainly would be sounder if these fragmentary, unrevised "extension courses," as Clarence Gohdes has called them, had been left in manuscript. When the opportunity for publication came, however, Mrs. Lanier readily consented, for she was desperately poor and had four children to bring up.

Although Lanier might have modified or developed his critical judgments and undoubtedly would have sharpened his style, it is unlikely that he would have made drastic changes if he had lived to prepare the manuscripts of *The English Novel* and *Shakspere and his Forerunners* for the press. The works express his convictions with more violence and less balance than finished works might do, but they grew out of and they reveal his thought, his prejudices, and his profound convictions. For this reason, these books and his other criticism are worth examination.

Although Sidney Lanier believed that "as a people, the novel is educating us," he had little interest in it as an art-form. He made the point to the group to whom he gave the misleadingly-entitled series of lectures, *The English Novel* (1881); to illustrate his point, he exhibited a copy of Henry James's *The American,* "which I borrowed the other day from the Mercantile Library, and which . . . certainly bears more marks of 'circulation' than any solid book in it." This education was not necessarily a good or moral one: Scott and Dickens and George Eliot used "this means to purify the air in one place while Zola in another applies the very same means to defiling the whole earth and slandering all humanity" (IV, 4–5). He approached reluctantly and belatedly the "unsavory muck" in which the roots of the English novel seemed to him imbedded. He dismissed them briefly. Richardson's *Pamela* was of less value as "a warning to young servant-girls" than as "an encouragement to old villains . . . instead of the title *Pamela: or Virtue Rewarded,* ought not the book to have been called *Mr. B.: or Villainy Rewarded?*" (IV, 147, 151).

He was equally severe on Richardson's later novels, and on those of Fielding and Smollett. Sterne's *Tristram Shandy* gave him more trouble: "I know good people who love the book; but to me, when you sum it all up, its teaching is that a man may spend his life in low, brutish, inane pursuits, and may have a good many little private sins on his conscience—but will nevertheless be sure of heaven if he can have retained the ability to weep a maudlin tear over a tale of distress." He could read none of these books by the four so-called classic novelists "without feeling as if my soul had been in the rain, draggled, muddy, miserable" and he sternly concludes that "if I had my way with these classic books I would blot them from the face of the earth" (IV, 156–157).

He could find only one "snowdrop springing from this muck of the classics"—Goldsmith's *Vicar of Wakefield.* Yet even it was minor: "No great work in the English novel appears until we reach Scott, whose *Waverley* astonished the world in 1814; and during the intervening period from this back to the *Vicar of Wakefield* perhaps there are no works notable enough to be mentioned in so rapid a sketch as this unless it be the society novels of Miss Burney, *Evelina* and *Cecilia,* the dark and romantic Mysteries-of-Udolpho stories of Mrs. Radcliffe, the *Caleb Williams* of William Godwin—with which he believed he was making an epoch because it was a novel without love as a motive—Miss Edgeworth's moral tales, and the quiet and elegant narratives of Jane Austen" (IV, 158–159).

This chaotic jumbling and judgment (or misjudgment) of novelists indicate that he had little concern for the form of the novel. This is borne out by his treating Elizabeth Barrett Browning's narrative poem *Aurora Leigh* as though it were one of the world's great novels and quoting from it extensively, and by his describing Erasmus Darwin's *The Loves of the Plants* (also in poetry) as "practically a series of little novels in which the heroes and heroines belong to the vegetable world." He was willing for this extension of genres to go both ways: he was not certain that poems would not be better if printed without artificial line divisions.

His own practice is even more conclusive. When his

father and his uncle objected to direct personal comments on contemporaries instead of through characters in *Tiger-Lilies,* Lanier omitted or watered them down, but he extended his answer so that it became a defense of the novel as a personal communication: "in regard to *the propriety of expressing individual opinions of the Author in other ways besides the utterances* of the characters in the book— I think perhaps you have failed to appreciate the distinctive feature of the *Novel,* as contrasted with the *Drama.* The difference between these two great methods of delineating events is, simply and only, that the Novel permits its Author to explain, by his *own mouth,* the 'situation': whereas, in the Drama, this must be done by the characters." Lanier believed that his conviction had been amply proved "by Authorities and precepts without number. The epigrammatic apophthegms of Victor Hugo; the polished man-of-the-world's advice of Bulwer; the erratic 'Extra-Leaves' of Jean Paul; the shallow but good-natured moralizings of G. P. R. James; the shrewd old-man's talks of Thackeray; the vigorous sermonizings of Mrs. Browning,—all these attest the legality of the expression, by the Novel-writer, of his own opinions" (VII, 231–232).

Acting on precedents that confirmed his own belief, Lanier did not hesitate to use the well-worn phrase "gentle reader," and somewhat coyly, though as it turned out over-optimistically, to tell his 24,999 readers how to interpret a particular situation (V, 7, 23).

Lanier did not believe that *Tiger-Lilies* was a great novel; he claimed only that he was justified in making it a vehicle for personal comment. The great English novelists of his own century, he reiterated, had done this. True, Scott had discussed no moral problems, but his redeeming trait was that his novels remained "always young, always healthy, always miraculous." But it was Scott's successors, those novelists who had grown to literary maturity be-

tween 1827 and 1857, who seemed superior to Richardson, Fielding, and Sterne. With some regret he dismissed
Bulwer, although admitting "that every novel of Bulwer's
is skillfully written and entertaining, and that there is not
an ignoble thought or impure stimulus in the whole
range of his works." He narrowed his list to six: Dickens,
Thackeray, Tennyson *(The Princess)*, Mrs. Browning
(Aurora Leigh), Charlotte Brontë, and George Eliot (V,
162–163).

He had reservations about Dickens and Thackeray. Essentially Dickens was a preacher and reformer who enlisted a great train of followers to do his bidding, yet kept
them "roaring with the genialest of laughter at the comi-
cal and grotesque figures which this preacher Dickens has
fished up out of the London mud." Thackeray mercilessly
exposed "sham and high vulgarity and minute wicked-
ness," but he was at best a somewhat slack and low-
pitched satirist, unworthy of Charlotte Brontë's fervent
admiration. Miss Brontë was intense and high-pitched;
Mrs. Browning and Tennyson were great and moral writers of fiction. But there was no question in Lanier's mind
that George Eliot was the greatest of English novelists,
and quite possibly the greatest of English writers since
Shakspere.

Part of this quality in her work grew out of her "intense feeling for personality." She combined poetic toler-
ance and scientific accuracy to gain a remarkable insight
in her perception of human beings. Where Dickens used
"rapid cartoon-strokes" that often approached "dangerously near to caricature," the marvel of George Eliot's art
was that, "though so cool and analytic, it nevertheless sets
before us perfect living flesh-and-blood people by fusing
the whole analytic process with a synthetic fire of the true
poet's human sympathy." She dealt mainly with unre-
markable persons, yet "with what delicious fun, what play

of wit, what ever-abiding and depth-illuminating humor, what creative genius, what manifold forms of living flesh and blood George Eliot preached the possibility of such moral greatness on the part of every most commonplace man and woman as completely reduces to a level the apparent inequality in the matter of genius" (V, 163–179).

The characters in *Middlemarch* seemed so real to the Laniers that after reading it he called his wife Dorothea and "when she is in a good humor, calls me Will Ladislaw . . . and when she is in a bad, addresses me as Mr. Casaubon." In that novel George Eliot had been "at once large and keen, at once broad and incisive"; it was a noble work and "about the best product of our times." To some degree, the changing mental climate was responsible for the book's superiority. Eliot could work with complex human personality in a way unknown to Aeschylus or even to Shakspere. She had also the incalculable advantage of working in "a freer form than the dramatic which arises from the more complex relations between modern personalities and which has really developed the novel out of the drama." This gave the novelist a chance to let the reader know "through moralizing comment and direct narrative a thousand things which the actor could not naturally tell us," and this above all lifted the novel to "the very highest and holiest plane of creative effort". (VIII, 345–346; IV, 5, 220–222). Even so, he preferred poetry to prose fiction.

Clifford Lanier described his brother's early poems as "*Byronesque*," but there is little in Sidney's surviving poems and nothing in his criticism to indicate that this influence was more than transitory. In *Tiger-Lilies* he used "The Destruction of Sennacherib" as the starting point for some elaborate punning, but his only lukewarm praise is that Byron in *Manfred* had "fairly translated" part of Aeschylus's *Prometheus Bound.* He paid grudging admiration to Coleridge, who lazily and without apparent effort had anticipated many of the ideas and expressions Lanier had thought original with himself; but Shelley he dismissed as having always "labored under an essential immaturity; it is very possible that if he had lived a hundred years he would never have become a man." Wordsworth he admired, although he thought it ironical that the English poet was rejected by ordinary readers and cherished most highly by "Matthew Arnold, the high-priest of culture." Of the early Romantic poets, only John Keats (in a youthful poem called his "dearest friend") continued to exert a powerful influence on his poetic and critical thinking: Lanier thought his "Ode to Melancholy" perhaps "reaches the highest height yet touched in the lyric line" (V, 151; IV, 69; I, 225–226; IV, 90; IV, 40, 44; I, 228; IV, 84).

His preference was for much earlier or for more nearly contemporary poets. He never doubted that Shakspere was the greatest of poets, or that Chaucer was second only to him in the line of English poets. His use of Shaksperean imagery is so close-knit and extensive that one unfamiliar with *Othello* could make little of "Night and Day," and one without acquaintance with *The Tempest* could make nothing of "Marsh Song—At Sunset." Yet Lanier was neither a logical nor a consistent critic. In *Shakspere and his Forerunners* he declared roundly that "Shakspere's work *is* moral teaching; it is all pure morality; every play *is,* in the strictest sense, a powerful sermon" (III, 186). In spite of this statement, he was troubled by the numerous indecencies in the plays, and in his poem "The Crystal" Lanier found it necessary to forgive Shakspere's bawdiness.

When he treated the plays, his method was comparatively simple. He trusted his own reading to make a threefold division: the dream period of youth, with *A Midsummer Night's Dream* as the most representative; the real or inquiring middle period, with *Hamlet* as the best embodiment of this spirit of inquiry; and the late ideal period, with *The Tempest* revealing a "supreme moral goodness" and sense of forgiveness of nature and of fate. For approximate datings and for the prevalence of end-stopped lines in the early plays and of run-on lines in the later ones, he relied on what seemed to him the best authorities of his time, although he did some independent checking of rhymes and versification. These three tests (moral content, historical datings, and metrical) justified his selection of the three plays as representative of the three great periods in Shakspere's life (IV, 326).

Although he thought *Beowulf* "substantially the oldest English poem," with a revelation of a new world of English beauty to those who studied it, and in his later poetry was strongly influenced by Anglo-Saxon alliteration, Lanier was disturbed that in it Nature was a rigorous monster "rendering and devouring the sons of men." By Shakspere's time the concept had changed: "The mood of Nature has become finer and sweeter, her fancy has abandoned the old savagery and revels in forms of unspeakable beauty." When Nature was regarded as simply physical and not as a manifestation of God on earth, it was inferior; Lanier constructed a triangle to illustrate the three main directions in which the poetic spirit looks:

$$\uparrow \text{God}$$
$$| \qquad \longrightarrow \text{Man}$$
$$\downarrow \text{Nature}$$

It was Shakspere who first markedly changed this concept of Nature; it was Wordsworth and Tennyson who revolutionized it (III, 26–27, 41).

Some of his judgments were highly personal, if not indeed capricious. Of Chaucer's poem *The Flower and the Leaf*, he stated unequivocally: "which I do not hesitate to pronounce a far finer poem than any of the *Canterbury Tales*—in fact, to my thinking, worth all the *Canterbury Tales* put together. One will look long in the literature of any land to find a picture of the deep woods in Spring painted with such fresh and vital and uplifting color, and conveyed in such marvellous easy words that seem to follow along after each other by some limpid necessity" (III, 29). True, he was contrasting the cheerfulness of *The Flower and the Leaf* with the grimness of *Beowulf*, and using Chaucer's poem as an intermediary between the harshness of the Anglo-Saxon literary point of view and the gentle humaneness of *A Midsummer Night's Dream*—but his immediate enthusiasm hardly justifies his uncritical judgment.

However, when he prepared a course and began preparation of a book that would compare three works each of Chaucer and of Shakspere, he turned unhesitatingly to the *Canterbury Tales* and selected "The Knight's Tale" to parallel *A Midsummer Night's Dream*, "The Pardoner's Tale" to parallel *Hamlet*, and "The Clerk's Tale" to parallel *The Tempest*. Lanier especially admired Chaucer as a craftsman: it can "be said that he has no obscure sentences, no complex or slovenly thoughts, no unrhythmic lines, and no bad rimes." Chaucer's language, he thought, presented no special difficulties once the reader realized that it was an intermingling of Anglo-Saxon and of French, with the pronunciation of vowels in the rimes strongly influenced by French usage. Once a few differences were recognized, the ability to read Chaucer's work in the original was easily acquired. Lanier thought this worth the effort (IV, 304, 335–37, 342).

When he planned an anthology of books of early English poets, Lanier listed one volume by Edmund Spenser.

Yet he reveals little personal enthusiasm for Spenser's poetry. In spite of quotations and allusions that testify to his own familiarity with it, he confessed that it required "both fortitude and reverence" for a complete reading of *The Faerie Queene.* He praised the smoothness of the verse in this poem and in the Amoretti sonnet-sequence (it "purls along like a little crystal stream gliding over the green polished stems of the watergrass"), but he disconcertingly thought that Spenser, "though more smooth and fluent than Daniel, is distinctly less large and noble in demeanor." And Spenser was so fond of antiquarian language that *The Faerie Queene* "often seems written nearer the time of King Edward III, than that of Queen Elizabeth" (X, 132; III, 5, 108, 129; IX, 397).

A large part of his enthusiasm for Elizabethan poetry Lanier reserved for the sonnet-writers. After a lengthy roll-call of those he considered good (twenty-seven in all), he announced that he would consider only six: Drummond, Constable, Daniel, Drayton, Sidney, and Shakspere. In fact, he also treated at some length, with buttressing quotations, the work of Wyatt, Surrey, and William Habington; he digresses to compare favorably a sonnet by Henry Timrod with one by Sidney; he quotes with approval Wordsworth's dictum that through the sonnet various great poets had unlocked their hearts. Sonnets seemed to Lanier to have several peculiar virtues: they were in the main poems of man's love for woman, not a frivolous but a manly, brave, and tender love; the sonnet brings the reader into an intimate relation with the writer: "When you read a sonnet of Shakspere's, it is as if you read a letter from him to you marked *confidential* at the top." Also, the good sonnet must by its nature be musical (III, 93–96).

Lanier was a rarity among the critics of his time in preferring the English or so-called illegitimate sonnet to the stricter Italian or legitimate form. Each sonnet should have one central idea; each should be a miniature drama complete in itself; each should be like "a flash of lightning in a dark night." He considered the rimed couplet at the end an advantage instead of a disadvantage; it unified the minor ideas with the central informing idea, and the concluding "antithesis of rime with rime affords an opportunity for a sharp and epigrammatic breaking off of the action." Wyatt had introduced the sonnet-form into English, but his language and versification were rough, and he limited himself to the division into eight and six lines with a change or turn between the parts. Surrey, by loosening the form and employing the rimed couplet at the end, was the true father of the English sonnet, as he was of English blank verse (III, 103–107).

Ben Jonson asserted to William Drummond of Hawthornden that the sonnet was a Procrustean bed which caused some poems to be either too long or too short. Lanier many years later accused him of having launched a tirade against the sonnet. The enforced brevity was a virtue, not a vice. Who today reads Daniel's *Musophilus*, Drayton's *Polyolbion* ("I could cite you a score of Drayton's sonnets any one of which will outweigh, in the dainty balances of art, the whole ponderous thirty thousand lines of the *Polyolbion*"), Sidney's *Arcadia*, or even Spenser's *Faerie Queene*. Instead of digressing, the poet is "obliged to mould his sonnet upon the form of the drama; and this very obligation of form, instead of being a hindrance . . . is a help and a salvation in holding the poet straight as an arrow-flight to the central conception of the poem." Daniel and Constable succeeded in the shorter form, although the latter's over-use of conceits offended many modern readers. Reversing a youthful judgment, Lanier declared that he was "not so afraid of conceits as some people," and that many readers, if they would allow themselves to do so, could enjoy these wild flights of the imagination. In comparing his love poets, Daniel seemed the lover of most dignity, Constable of the nimblest fancy, and Habington the happiest since he continued to write sonnets to his lady after she became his wife (III, 123–124, 135).

By contrast, Sidney and Shakspere, the greatest of English sonneteers, were far more intensely subjective. Lanier agreed that *Astrophel to Stella* is "really a record of his passion for Lady Rich" and that many were written after she had married Lord Rich, but he objected to the interpretation of some biographers that this suggested an illicit relationship. With his usual emphasis on morality, Lanier insisted that the sonnets, intended only for her eyes, actually refute any such accusation, and he quotes five to prove his point. In the same way, he accepts that the first part of Shakspere's sonnet-sequence was written to a man, but he apparently never harbored the idea that these might indicate a latent or an active homosexuality; instead, he had lavished his affection upon a man who had betrayed him. It is a manly friendship, and nothing more. The woman he loved was likewise unfaithful, transferring her love to his friend. These are incomparable poems, but only in the life of Beethoven does one find an equal betrayal of a supreme artist—and Lanier speculated inconclusively that perhaps great works of art grew out of darkness and winter rather than out of sunlight and springtime (III, 154–156).

His reading of Elizabethan sonnets led to one rather strange enthusiasm: Bartholomew Griffin's sequence to Fidessa. They were entitled, he thought, "to take their place in our regard beside the *Amoretti* of Spenser, the *Idea* of Drayton, the sonnets of Daniel to Delia, of Sidney to Stella, of William Drummond to his short-lived lady." To Lanier, Griffin proved that the English idiom ran

easily into the mould of the sonnet, but his special characteristic was to mingle a despairing lover's cry with a ro-
guish conscience of the absurdity of the situation. But
Lanier admitted, and his numerous quotations bear him
out, that Griffin was guilty of a childlike naïveté and
simplicity (IV, 276).

For Milton, as for Dante and Goethe, he had little
affection. He wondered why it was Milton and not Shakspere who had "treated the subject of Paradise Lost and
Regained; how is it that the first-class subject was left for
the second-class genius?" (IV, 223). Milton had failed in
what he intended, for the only character "which has taken
a real hold upon the world is his Satan." He objected also
when Milton portrayed Shakspere as warbling his native
wood-notes wild: "this description betrays a conception of
Shakspere about as appropriate as one that should figure
Ralph Waldo Emerson as the canary-bird of American
Song" (III, 166). Emerson stimulated Lanier's thinking
and influenced his writing, but it was the Emerson of the
Essays, not of the Poems.

Milton must be reckoned with, but most of the poets
who followed him could be disregarded. Dryden (with
Wordsworth) is once rebuked for his "wretched redactions" of Chaucer; in a more thoughtful and extended
objection to translations in general, Lanier moderated his
censure; after noting that only the great poems in the
Bible could bear translation from one language to another
without hurt, he added:

> how pitiful is Homer as he appears even in Pope's Eng-
> lish; or how subtly does the simplicity of Dante melt into
> childishness even with Mr. Longfellow guiding; or how
> tedious and flat fall the cultured sentences of Goethe
> even in Taylor's version, which has by many been de-
> clared the most successful translation ever made, not only
> of Faust but of any foreign poem; nay, how completely
> the charm of Chaucer exhales away even when redacted

merely from an older dialect into a later one, by hands
so skillful as those of Dryden and Wordsworth! (IV, 336,
240)

This is a legitimate objection, but it seems odd that
Lanier with his love for music never once mentioned
Dryden's "Alexander's Feast; or, the Power of Music."

In general, the poetry of the Dryden-Pope school
seemed to him stilted, wooden, and monotonous. Thus,
Pope, although using the same line as blank verse,
"drones through page after page. . . . The lines move two
and two, by inexorable couplets, like charity-school children in procession, each pair holding hands; and the
exactness becomes presently intolerable to the modern
ear." Probably for this reason, although he approved the
moral tone of *Rasselas,* he had no use for Samuel John-
son's poetry (III, 340).

He enjoyed ballads. One of his books for boys is a sim-
plified selection from Thomas Percy's *Reliques of Ancient
English Poetry* and from other collections. Lanier was a
conscientious editor, although he noted that "the spelling
has been modernized and such parts cut away as clean-
liness required." The manly ballads were a useful anti-
dote to the dandified poems of men like Matthew Prior,
whom Lanier could not forgive for prettifying in "Henry
and Emma" his own favorite, the "Nut Browne Mayde."
He thought its language an "almost perfect specimen of
simple, pathetic, strong, unaffected English." Genuine ballads like this and the stories of Robin Hood had a clear
beauty; they were unaffected and healthy; they portrayed
honest emotions honestly. As works of literature, they had
helped to rescue English poetry from the "silly, affected
and insincere" works of the late eighteenth century. Even
more important, in life, "poetry in the disguise of a ballad
or common minstrel often steals through the hard battle
of men's lives bringing subtle news of reinforcement from
unseen friends" (IV, 382–397; II, 91–92).

When Virginia Hankins in 1875 wrote him that she still believed in "the masterhood of Tennyson and William Morris," Lanier advised her rather sharply that these were not the finest models for an aspiring poet: "No, Tennyson and William Morris are not the masters; indeed, My Child, they never were: and it is the goodness of your heart, together with the poetry of your own which you unconsciously put between their lines, that have made you think so. Chaucer and Shakspere—these are the Masters" (IX, 232–233). For all this advice, Lanier himself was more influenced by Tennyson than by any other poet except Shakspere; he thought Tennyson the best and noblest of contemporary poets. Lanier believed that modern poetry was more ethereal than that of past times, and that Tennyson's poetry was more spiritual than Milton's. As the early poets presented it, Nature rose only half-way to the dignity of man, but when Tennyson poetically "strolls into a glen, the *genus loci* is now not a hamadryad but a veritable human soul." Thus Nature, humanized and spiritualized, became through Tennyson and other modern poets "a genuine companion and friend of man" (V, 285–286, 297).

Although in *The Science of English Verse* Lanier frequently used Tennyson's poems to illustrate his theories of musical scansion and set several of Tennyson's poems to music, he made a significant qualification. After praising highly the musical and melodious quality of Paul Hamilton Hayne's verse, he added: "It is, in this respect, simply unique in modern poetry: Wm Morris comes nearest to it, but Morris lives too closely within hearing of Tennyson to write unbroken music: for Tennyson (let me not blaspheme against the Gods!) is not a musical tho' in other respects (particularly in that of phrase-making) a very wonderful writer." This was his one defect. *In Memoriam* proved beyond cavil that science was not inimical to poetry, but a strength and an aid: "science, instead of being

the enemy of poetry, is its quartermaster and commissary
—it forever purveys for poetry." Tennyson's *Princess*,
with its noble idea of marriage, proved his own age more
civilized than the age represented in Plato's *Republic*. To
justify his somewhat uneasy feeling about writing dialect
poems, he wrote to Virginia Hankins that "One must remember that Burns wrote almost wholly in dialect: and
that the strongest poem of Tennyson ["Northern Farmer,
Old Style"] is in dialect." Writing about his projected
Boy's King Arthur, Lanier listed as one reason for antici-
pating its success the fact that "It is from Malory's book
that Tennyson drew the stories which he has woven into
his *magnum opus*—the *Idylls of the King*" (VIII, 347;
IV, 34–39; V, 321; IX, 203; see also 208; X, 109).

   Although he once called Robert Browning "my master
and dear reverend poet," Lanier was troubled by the difficult, unmusical style. In 1870 he wrote to Hayne:

> Have you seen Browning's "The Ring and the Book"?
> I am confident that, at the birth of this man, among all
> the good fairies who showered him with magnificent en-
> dowments, one bad one—as in the old tale—crept in by
> stealth and gave him a constitutional twist i' the neck,
> whereby his windpipe became, and has remained ever
> since, a marvellous tortuous passage. Out of this glottis-
> labyrinth his words won't, and can't, come straight. . . .
> You get lightning-glimpses—and, as one naturally ex-
> pects from lightning, zigzag glimpses—into the intense
> night of the passion of these souls. It is entirely wonder-
> ful and without precedent.

Browning's poetry was like an expertly-thrown lasso, with
a thousand coils and turns, but at the end the noose was
directly in front of the bison's head (IX, 49; VIII,
72–73).

   He had no such reservations about the poetry of Elizabeth Barrett Browning. With his usual indifference to
form, he compared her narrative poem *Aurora Leigh* fa-

vorably with the novels of George Eliot; the works of the two women delightfully complemented, although they did not duplicate, each other. In that poem and in the *Drama of Exile* she presented a lofty concept of morality, and she revealed human beings becoming wise through grief, love, and forgiveness, but especially through love. Only through love could an ideal beauty come, and only with love could it be presented. He approved of what he called her "vigorous sermonizings" on these subjects, for they tallied with his own beliefs (IV, 132, 187, 200, 235; VII, 232).

His feelings about William Morris as poet underwent a marked sea-change. He wrote to Virginia Hankins in 1869 that for a birthday present he had given his wife the *Earthly Paradise:* "She has been reading some of it to me, in my sick moments. It is very *great*. It is good for *you* to read. It is simple, *toned down,* strong, unstrained, dreamy, real, sensuous, pure, and *good*. Read all the stories. You will like them better, the more you know them." By 1875, when his article on Hayne's poems finally appeared, this unstinted enthusiasm had been drastically reduced. He praised Hayne's skillful handling of the sonnet-form in "To William Morris," but he objected vigorously and at disproportionate length (considering his subject) when Hayne concluded that Morris was the one true heir of Chaucer. Although "we owe some keen delights to Mr. Morris," Lanier dissented from the opinion that any comparison between the two could be justified:

> how does the spire of hope spring and upbound into the infinite of Chaucer; while, on the other hand, how blank, world-bound, and wearying is the stone *façade* of hopelessness which rears itself uncompromisingly behind the gayest pictures of William Morris. . . .
>
> Again, how openly joyful is Chaucer; how secretly melancholy is Morris! Both, it is true, are full of sunshine; but Chaucer's is spring-sunshine, Morris's is

autumn. . . . Chaucer lives, Morris dreams. Chaucer, for
all the old-world tales he tells, yet tells them with the
mouths and manners of his living time, and so gives us a
picture of it like life itself. Morris stands between his
people and his readers, interpreting his characters, who all
advance to the same spot on the stage, communicate *per*
him in the same language, the same dialect, the same tone,
then glide away with the same dreamy mechanism. . . .

And finally . . . note the faith that shines in Chaucer
and the doubt that darkens in Morris. Has there been
any man since St. John so lovable as "the Persoune"? or
any sermon since that on the Mount so keenly analytical,
so pathetic, so deep, so pitiful, so charitable, so pure, so
manly, so faithful, so hopeful, so sprightly, so terrible, so
childlike, so winning, so utterly loving as *The Persoune's
tale?* . . . there is no man since Shakspere who has been
at all capable of *that*.

His mature opinion he summed up in a Poem Outline:

WILLIAM MORRIS
He caught a crystal cup-full of the yellow light of sunset,
and, persuading himself to dream it wine, drank it with
a sort of smile (V, 322–325; I, 260).

And in the same group of projected but never written
poems, Lanier wrote of Swinburne that "He invited me
to eat, the service was silver and gold, but no food therein
save pepper and salt," and that "It is always the Fourth of
July with Mr. Swinburne. It is impossible, in reading this
strained laborious matter, not to remember that this case
of poetry is precisely that where he who conquers conquers without strain." Dr. Edwin Mims has justly pointed
out that this last statement is equally applicable to much
of Lanier's own poetry.

An early and enduring influence on Lanier's thought
was the poetry and criticism of Edgar Allan Poe. True,
late in his life he resented the imputation that *The Science of English Verse* was based on the ideas in Poe's

"Rationale of Verse" and thought that Poe "did not *know*
enough" to be a great poet—but this judgment, as Charles
R. Anderson has perceptively noted, was made after
Lanier "had come to think of the poet as a religious seer,
'in charge of all learning to convert it into wisdom' (II,
6)—a theory quite opposite from Poe's." But the perva-
sive influence of Poe, with his mood of melancholy, can be
traced in Lanier's youthful poetry, and the continuing
influence of Poe's technique is easily apparent in "Song of
the Chattahoochee." In 1863 he advised Mary Day to read
Poe's *Eureka* for its "beautiful extension" of Laplace's
nebular theory of the cosmogony: "I have often thought it
. . . a beautiful description of the way a Soul gets filled
with thoughts and feelings" (I, xxiv n., xxxv–xxxvi; X,
204; VII, 95).

Lanier's first literary friend was Paul Hamilton Hayne,
though the two met only through correspondence (Lanier
knew John Banister Tabb in the Federal prison at Point
Lookout, but their friendship then seems to have been
based more on music than on poetry). Always generous-
hearted, Hayne initiated the correspondence in 1868 after
reading a lyric that he liked, and he consistently praised
Lanier's poems, even fragments of "The Jacquerie" that
were sent to him. Lanier was not always equally generous.
When Hayne sent a manuscript copy of "Fire-Pictures,"
Lanier returned it with the comment that "I have picked
out a grain or two of gravel, as it were, and slag," then
suggested no less than nine revisions, most of them sensible but two or three niggling, and one that would have
destroyed the unity of the poem. Quite early, Lanier considered himself the better poet and therefore felt himself
qualified to recommend textual and structural changes.
Yet he sincerely admired "Fire-Pictures", a poem which
"in point of variety and delicacy of fancy is quite the best
of this collection [*Legends and Lyrics*], and in point of
pure music should be placed beside Edgar Poe's *Bells*."

Lanier frequently commended the musical qualities of Hayne's verse (VIII, 145–148; V, 327).

He was likewise enthusiastic about the "entire *absence*, in everything you write, of *Trade* in any of its forms. Utterly *uncommercial:* that is glorious, my dear Friend, and that is the spirit of your writings." He returned indirectly to this praise in his article on Hayne's poetry: "in *Legends and Lyrics* we find no polemical discussion, no 'science,' no 'progress.'" Hayne was mindful only of "grand phenomena which no one doubts—of fear, hope, love, patriotism, heaven, wife, child, mother, clouds, sunlight, flowers, water" (VII, 223; V, 326). Although Lanier meant this as honest commendation, he was unwittingly drawing attention to a certain soft-mindedness in Hayne's (and in his own) poetry.

Since he thought Hayne's defects as poet remediable, Lanier publicly called attention to them. (It is interesting to note that he might have, but did not, apply these criteria to his own verse.) The first was "a frequently-recurring *lapsus* of thought, in which Mr. Hayne falls into trite similes, worn collocations of words and commonplace sentiments"; the second, "diffuseness, principally originating in a lavishness and looseness of adjectives." Poe's theory of brevity and tension might be open to question, but "the ideal of the lyric poem is a brief, sweet, intense, electric flashing of the lyric idea in upon the hurrying intelligence of men" (V, 329–330).

Rather oddly, Lanier also objected to Hayne's antiquarianism. When Chaucer wrote "The Frankeleine's Tale," men had not "really settled in their minds whether it was right to break even a criminal oath, made in folly." But this concept belonged to the past; in a modern re-writing like "The Wife of Brittany," it was only a curiosity of history. Chaucer wrote of a real passion and terror, but Hayne wrote "under the disadvantage of feeling at the bottom of his heart that the passion of the poem is amateur passion, the terror of it amateur terror, and the whole business little more than a dainty titillation of the unreal" (V, 326). Evidently Lanier did not read the poem discerningly: he never realized that Hayne was attempting to substitute a psychological for a magical basis.

In spite of this harsh, digressive, and partially unfair review of his poetry, Hayne did not break off the correspondence, but he allowed it to lag. When, however, Lanier in *Florida* described Henry Timrod as the author of spontaneous and delicate lyrics who "never had time to learn the mere craft of the poet—the technique of verse" (VI, 160–161), Hayne dissented sharply. Timrod was generally acknowledged to be a master craftsman, knowledgeable in matters of versification and of poetic techniques; he knew considerably more about these matters, Hayne at least hinted, than Lanier did. Perhaps by way of recompense, Lanier quoted and praised a Timrod sonnet in *Shakspere and his Forerunners.*

Friendship no doubt led him to over-estimate the value of Bayard Taylor's writings. He was grateful to Taylor for generous yet knowledgeable encouragement, for sane criticism, and for introducing him to prominent literary men. Yet there can be no question that his admiration was sincere. In comparing the concepts of personality in ancient and modern times, he selected as three suitable plays Aeschylus's *Prometheus Bound,* Shelley's *Prometheus Unbound,* and Taylor's *Prince Deukalion.* Taylor, in contrast with Aeschylus and more explicitly than Shelley, celebrated the development in modern times of spirituality and of personality; he had aimed to array before us the whole panorama of time, and at the end the union of Deukalion and Pyrra, the ideal man and the ideal woman. Lanier thought Taylor had succeeded in this drama of developing and developed personalities (IV, 66, 96–101, 145–146).

Yet Lanier was by no means a slavish admirer. When

Taylor sent a copy of his Centennial Hymn, Lanier suggested such wholesale changes that, if adopted would have necessitated re-writing the entire poem; Taylor thanked him, but answered drily that "I don't entirely agree with you in regard to a rigid architectural structure for the hymn. . . . Here again, is an instance where you cannot apply the laws of Music to Poetry." In the end, Whittier wrote the Hymn and Taylor the Ode. But Lanier did not give up the point. Taylor's weakness as poet was that, although every sentiment, thought, and line were exquisite, yet the whole did not give "a full white light *as poems* for want of a proper convergence of the components upon a single point." This was a discerning commentary not only on Taylor's poetry but on all his literary work (IX, 333–335; 344–345).

Lanier's literary relationship with John Banister Tabb was rather that of a mentor than of a critic. Thinking Tabb dead, when he admired the anonymously-published "The Cloud" in *Harper's,* it never occurred to him that Tabb was the author. In a letter asking for suggestions about his unpublished poem, "An Allegory," Tabb admitted being the author of the earlier poem. Lanier offered to send the new poem to J. G. Holland, editor of *Scribner's,* but recommended two changes: a less commonplace title, one that would be more attractive in the table of contents; and the dropping of the third and fourth verses. Tabb did not make either change, and Holland accepted "An Allegory" and "The Swallow," although Lanier objected strongly that "borne" and "on" were "not admissible as a rhyme." He was even more drastic in suggesting word-changes in "Repose," wanting less vigorous words that would give, not out-pourings, but "emanations, or the like subtle outgivings of placid Power." He also suggested changing the verse form from alternating four and two feet lines to a line of six feet with rhyming couplets because these long lines "have a very peculiar *repose* in their placid movement" (IX, 465–466; 469–470; 505–507).

Lanier did not read *Leaves of Grass* until the spring of 1878, in a copy borrowed from Bayard Taylor. Ordering a copy for himself, he wrote to Walt Whitman: "Although I entirely disagree with you in all points connected with artistic form, and in so much of your doctrine as is involved in those poetic exposures of the person which your pages so unreservedly make, yet I feel sure that I understand you therein, and my dissent in these particulars becomes a very insignificant consideration in the presence of that unbounded delight which I take in the bigness and bravery of all your ways and thoughts" (X, 40). The two objections expressed here continued to qualify his enthusiasm. Lanier disclaimed and condemned "that flippant and sneering tone which dominates so many discussions of Whitman," but he found it ironic that when Whitman abandoned his theory of formlessness he had in "O Captain, My Captain" written "one of the most tender and beautiful poems in any language." Equally ironic was the fact that Whitman claimed to be the poet of democracy and of democrats, but his poetry (like Wordsworth's) could be read only by people of sophisticated taste. Such poetry "would be impossible except in a highly civilized state of society."

Lanier continued to be troubled also by what seemed to him false claims for manliness and freedom: "I cannot close these hasty remarks upon the Whitman school without a fervent protest, in the name of all arts and all artists, against a poetry which has painted a great sprawling figure of the human body and has written under it, '*This is the soul.*'" True religion, Lanier felt, did not mean abandoning oneself to every passion or even to naturalness (IV, 39–54).

He wrote outlines for two poems, never written, that apparently were to sum up his basic objections: "Whitman is poetry's butcher. Huge raw collops slashed from the rump of poetry and never mind gristle, is what Whitman feeds our souls with." "As near as I can make it out, Whitman's argument seems to be that because a prairie is wide, therefore debauchery is admirable, and because the Mississippi River is long, therefore every American is God" (I, 260–261).

Aubrey Starke thought the weaknesses in Lanier's criticism could be traced to "enthusiasm, lack of catholicity of judgment, and didacticism" (441). These are important, but they need to be more closely defined and delimited. Enthusiasm led him to over-praise good writers like Tennyson and George Eliot, and mediocre writers like Bartholomew Griffin. In part, however, this over-enthusiasm and with it a lack of catholicity grew out of Lanier's belief that matter constantly etherealizes, and that the great development of modern times was the emphasis on individuality and personality. Since Greek writers like Plato and Aeschylus seemed to him to have denied these values, he consistently underestimated and sometimes denigrated their work. It was this change in values that led Lanier to set Tennyson above Milton—certainly a defect in taste. Sometimes his enthusiasms were mystical rather than rational, as when he proclaimed Bishop Aldhelm the father of English poetry when none of Aldhelm's poems in English have survived. And perhaps it is less didacticism than a high yet narrow, prudish morality that blinded him to the value of writers like Fielding, Sterne, and Zola, and made the idea of "Art for Art's Sake" repugnant to him. These qualities reveal an immaturity of thought and a lack of logical reasoning that weaken his criticism (IV, 227, 232 ff.).

Yet his enthusiasm is also a critical strength. The commentaries on Chaucer and Shakspere and George Eliot do illuminate their works for later readers; more important, these enthusiasms and flashes of insight do entice readers to go back to the originals. If his moral standards were unduly narrow, they were at least grounded in the firm ethical belief, as he advised young artists, that "unless you are suffused—body and soul, one might say—with that moral purpose which finds its largest expression in love— that is, the love of all things in their proper relation— unless you are suffused with this love, do not dare to meddle with beauty; unless you are suffused with beauty, do not dare to meddle with love; unless you are suffused with truth, do not dare to meddle with goodness,—in a word, unless you are suffused with beauty, truth, wisdom, goodness, *and* love, abandon the hope that the ages will accept you as an artist" (IV, 239). These superhuman qualities Lanier demanded in the work of other writers and he attempted to embody them in his own poems.

Soon after *The Science of English Verse* (1880) was published, Lanier recognized its inadequacy and was eager to revise it (X, 195)—another project that came to nothing because of his early death. He indicated no dissatisfaction with the title, which has proved a stumbling-block to readers in his own and later times. He used the word *verse* in its narrow sense of metrical or prosodical versification, although admitting that in common usage it often meant a stanza, in its classic sense a line, and frequently to denominate a slight or inferior poetry. He was concerned almost exclusively with sound, or the appeal to the ear; he does not treat at all the image, or appeal to the eye; and he mentions only in passing emotion or thought, or the appeal to the mind, as when he admits that "in Shakspere's verse the only way to get the exact rhythm is to read for the sense." He had written a technical treatise in what he hoped were clear and non-technical terms, so that it seemed "at once a popular treatise and a general student's handbook" (II, 167, 187; X, 197).

The word *science* proved even more confusing than *verse*. Could versification be reduced to an exact or a single formula when over the centuries excellent poems had been written by men who at least thought they were writing accentual or quantitative or free verse? Poets and critics alike objected that the writing of poetry was an art, not a science. Lanier with some reason was perturbed and incensed, for he felt that he had "set up the sharpest distinction between Verse and Poetry—between mere Technic and Inspiration," and he denied that he had prescribed how poems should be written. In his brief conclusion Lanier conceded that he had given only hints as to poetic form: "For the artist in verse there is no law: the perception and love of beauty constitute the whole outfit: and what is herein set forth is to be taken merely as enlarging that perception, and exalting that love. In all cases, the appeal is to the ear; but the ear should, for that purpose, be educated up to the highest possible plane of culture" (X, 204; II, xxxi, 244).

Apparently the book had its inception in a series of eight lectures delivered to a group of ladies in Baltimore in 1878, four on "The Science of Poetry" and four on the Elizabethan sonneteers. He expanded this material into three articles entitled "The Physics of Poetry," which *Scribner's Monthly* accepted but never published because Lanier desired to turn the material into "a complete Manual of English Prosody." Lanier, with unbounded enthusiasm, felt that in the three articles he had "put formal poetry on a scientific basis which renders all its processes perfectly secure." In a careful summary Paul F. Baum has sketched out the key ideas which Lanier developed more fully in his book. The first article, "Rhythm" begins by assuming that the form of a poem is a succession of sounds, that "while Sound is the *Form* of all poetry, it is the *Substance* of all Verse," and that these are "precisely the same" as those of music. This was his fundamental premise; since in general the longer, more finished work treats the same material in the same order, it seems only just to turn immediately to *The Science of English Verse.*

At the beginning Lanier insisted that the "term 'Verse' denotes a set of specially related sounds," and that "when we hear verse, we *hear* a set of relations between sounds; when we silently read verse, we *see* that which brings to us a set of relations between sounds; when we imagine verse, we *imagine* a set of relations between sounds" (II, 22, 23).

It was natural that Lanier, a musician, should have set the primary emphasis on the sound of words. But it seems odd that he never once mentioned the pictograph, or communication through the eye. He set an inordinate value on the human voice. Yet that voice, being human, is fallible and, more, variable. I have seen American-Japanese soldiers, when they wanted another person to be certain of their meaning, draw characters in the palm of the hand while they were speaking the words. Two skilled performers can reproduce almost exactly the same tones from a musical composition, if they forego the luxury of personal interpretation, for the basis of musical composition is grounded in the logic of mathematics. But words (although not necessarily all sounds) have been increasingly governed by the logic of rhetoric. I have yet to hear the human voice that could give exactly the same cadence or value to the five *nevers* in Shakspere's famous line or that could give equal value, as Lanier insisted was true, to the three syllables in the word *rhythm-ic-al.* Many modern dictionaries, recognizing this difficulty, divide the word into *rhyth-mi-cal.* But Lanier put his faith in the belief that speech, like music, was only one variant of sound.

On this assumption, he wrote with conviction that:

> Sounds may be studied with reference to four and only four, particulars. We may observe—
>
> (1) How long a sound lasts *(duration);*
> (2) How loud a sound is *(intensity);*
> (3) How shrill—that is, how high, as to bass or treble —a sound is *(pitch);*
> (4) Of what sounds a given sound is composed—for, as in studying colors we find purple composed of red and violet, and the like, so many sounds have been discovered to be made up of other sounds *(tone-color)* (II, 23).

Many students of English prosody, including Edgar Allan Poe, had made "a fundamental mistake" when they attempted to replace quantity with accent as the basis of English verse, under the erroneous belief that "the accent makes every syllable *long."* But verse depended on time, not on stress. Set in italic type for emphasis, he wrote that a *"formal poem is always composed of such sounds and silences . . . as can be co-ordinated by the ear."* There were, he believed, only three particulars as to which the human ear has the power of exactly co-ordinating sounds: duration, pitch, and tone-color (II, 11, 29, 32–35). Rhythm depended on duration, tune on pitch. Briefly he defined the similarities and the difference between verse and music:

> The art of verse, then, as well as the art of music,—the two species of the genus art of sound,—includes all the three great classes of phenomena summed up under the terms rhythm, tune, and tone-color. We will presently find many problems solved by the full recognition of this fact that there is absolutely no difference between the sound-relations used in music and those used in verse.
>
> If this be true,—if the sound-relations of music and verse are the same,—we are necessarily forced to look for

the difference between the two arts in the nature of the sounds themselves with which they deal. Here, indeed, the difference lies. Expressed, as far as possible, in popular terms, it is as follows:—

> When those exact co-ordinations which the ear perceives as rhythm, tune, and tone-color, are suggested to the ear by a series of *musical sounds,* the result is . . . . . . MUSIC
> When those exact co-ordinations which the ear perceives as rhythm, tune, and tone-color, are suggested to the ear by a series of *spoken words*, the result is . . . . . . VERSE (II, 41).

This held true even when the words were read silently, for print and writing are only "systems of notation for the tone-colors of the human speaking-voice."

Using musical notes for his system of scansion, Lanier examined many poems by such diverse writers as Queen Elizabeth, Shakspere, Tennyson, Poe, Caedmon, Chaucer, Coleridge, Keats, Swinburne, and Morris. This examination confirmed his belief that primary rhythm exists only through the co-ordination of time. Accent can effect nothing except to arrange materials already rhythmical through some temporal recurrence. The ear can supply a secondary rhythm, but only after a primary rhythm has been imposed.

The foot in verse, like the bar in music, is always exactly equal in time to any other foot, but there were methods of varying this symmetrical monotony. There were longer units that must be reckoned with; the varying effects of all these combine to exhibit to the ear,

> (1) The relative duration of each primary unit or individual verse-sound ("syllable") constituting what may be scientifically termed the first order of rhythm and what is commonly termed . . . . . . QUANTITY
> (2) The relative duration of each secondary unit, or individual group of verse-sounds (the bar, sometimes also called "measure," same as the classic "foot"), constituting

what may be scientifically termed the second order of rhythm and what is commonly termed . . . . . . RHYTHM

(3) The relative duration of each tertiary unit, or larger individual group of verse-sounds (the "phrase"), constituting what may be scientifically termed the third order of rhythm, which divides into . . . . . . THE PHRASE, THE ALLITERATIVE GROUP, AND THE EMPHATIC WORD GROUP

(4) The relative duration of each fourth-order unit, or still larger group of verse-sounds (the "line"), constituting what may be scientifically termed the fourth order of rhythm and what is commonly termed . . . . . . METRE

(5) The relative duration of each fifth-order unit, or still larger group of verse-sounds (the "stanza"), constituting what may be scientifically termed the fifth order of rhythm and what is commonly termed in English the verse or more correctly the . . . . . . STANZA

(6) The final rhythmic group embracing all these and called . . . . . . THE POEM (II, 76).

Although he continued to deny that accent was the basis of English prosody, Lanier readily admitted that it could not be disregarded. The function of accent was to call the ear's attention to particular sounds in a series; this could be done through rhythmic accent, pronunciation accent, or logical accent, or by a combination of these. But these were at best subsidiary aids; they confirmed rather than hindered his belief that all English verse was written in three forms of 3-rhythm and two forms of 4-rhythm: (1) the varied syllabication of Anglo-Saxon poetry, held together by alliteration on certain strong syllables; (2) the iambic, used by Chaucer and quickly becoming the main form in English verse, whether rhymed or unrhymed; in lines of five feet, it has become the most-used of English rhythmic forms; (3) the shifting of accent within the foot but keeping to 3/8 time; (4) the classic 4/8 dactyl, commonly with the emphasis on the first syllable; (5) the rarely-used spondee, with two equally long syllables (II, 94–97, 109).

Fascinated by what he considered a scientific way of dating Shakspere's plays and testifying to his belief in Shakspere's "miraculous" art in the management of blank verse, Lanier digresses at length to discuss the rhythmical use of the rest, of end-stopped and run-on lines, of double-ending or feminine-ending lines, and of weak-ending and light-ending lines. This amateur scholarship has long been superseded. More puzzling is the fact that Lanier barely mentions in passing the blank verse of John Milton, presenting no analysis of it at all (II, 145, 136, 144).

Since the book at its inception was linked with lectures on the Elizabethan sonneteers, it is not surprising that Lanier treated the sonnet separately, as his main example of the unifying force of the stanza. He accepted the division, standard in his day, into Italian or legitimate sonnets with stricter form and fewer rhyme-words, and the English or illegitimate sonnet with three quatrains and epigrammatic concluding couplet. Unlike Leigh Hunt and Paul Hamilton Hayne, he preferred the English type, calling it "really the primordial form of modern English lyric poetry" and "sacred to all serious people since the heavenly series of private prayers and confessions which Shakspere whispered in it" (II, 188–191).

Lanier dismissed tune briefly. Tune in speech consisted of verbal melody, of distinctly formulated patterns of tones varying in pitch. Even in ordinary speech these may change the signification and even modify the meaning of the same word. So poetry, in the desire to be independent of its sister-art, has come to rely less on music and more upon "the subtle and practicable tunes of the speaking-voice" (II, 197, 205).

Lanier approached tone-color more systematically:

> When the ear co-ordinates a series of verse-sounds with special reference to their tone-colors, the resulting perceptions may be considered under the following four di-

visions, which embrace most of such co-ordinations as are
of artistic importance in English verse, to wit:

(1) Rhyme: which involves both vowels and consonants;

(2) Vowel-distribution: which involves the consideration of vowels alone, with reference to securing agreeable
successions of them in the line;

(3) Consonant-distribution: which involves the consideration of consonants alone, with reference to *(a)* securing agreeable junctions of the terminal consonant of each
word with the initial consonant of the next word, and
with reference to *(b)* arranging pleasant recurrences of
similar consonant-colors;

(4) Alliteration: which involves both vowels and consonants (II, 219).

That rhyme had in English poetry a pleasing effect on
the ear he was quick to admit. Some manifestations occurred in Anglo-Saxon poetry. But rhyme had too often
been used as a substitute for exact words and good sense,
and too often the poet had been content with an approxi-
mation. Except in humorous or dialect poetry, this would
not do: "If the rhyme is not perfect, if it demands any the
least allowance, it is not tolerable: throw it away. . . .
The student may rest with confidence in the belief that
no rhyme but a perfect rhyme is ever worth a poet's
while." It is perhaps as well that Lanier was not familiar
with Emily Dickinson's poetry. He was more lenient in
the requirements about vowel-colors and consonant
distribution; once the good craftsman was aware of the
need for variety, no rules beyond the poet's judgment
need be given. As for alliteration, while the Anglo-Saxon
poet used it to "establish and fortify the main rhythm of
the verse, its effect in modern verse is to vary the main
rhythm by irregular and unlooked-for groups which break
the monotony of the set rhythmic movement" (II,
229–230, 239).

The book did not have the revolutionary effect on English prosody that Lanier hoped for. It has proved to be suggestive and stimulating, but in no sense definitive. A typical reaction was expressed in a letter from his fellow-poet E. C. Stedman that he preferred analysis after having written his poems "by instinct, than to attempt, *a priori*, to sing in accordance with laws which govern the poet willy-nilly" (X, 194). Lanier was justifiably incensed. The reviews were just as obtuse: "it is perfectly fair to say that nine out of ten, even of those which most generously treated the book in hand, treated it upon the general theory that a work on the science of verse must necessarily be a collection of rules for making verses. . . . In point of fact, a book of rules for making verses might very well be written, but then it would be a hand-book of the art of verse, and would take the whole science of verse for granted,—like an instruction-book for the piano, or the like" (IV, 30).

Lanier thought that he had established the scientific law of prosody. In his view, his position was diametrically opposite to that of Walt Whitman, who seemed to advocate and to practice a prosodical formlessness. Lanier wished to impose a scientific form on a previously loose and little-understood medium. But when in his own poetry the syllable *So* can be at once a foot and a line, when four light syllables can be run together as a foot, and when these poetic feet can be thrown together in one poem, the most noticeable and lasting result, ironically, is that Lanier, like Whitman, helped mightily to loosen up the technique of English versification.

Index